Perl Programming for Beginners

An Introduction to Learn Perl Programming with Tutorials and Hands-On Examples

Legal & Disclaimer

The information contained in this book and its contents is not designed to replace or take the place of any form of medical or professional advice; and is not meant to replace the need for independent medical, financial, legal or other professional advice or services, as may be required. The content and information in this book has been provided for educational and entertainment purposes only.

The content and information contained in this book has been compiled from sources deemed reliable, and it is accurate to the best of the Author's knowledge, information, and belief. However, the Author cannot guarantee its accuracy and validity and cannot be held liable for any errors and/or omissions. Further, changes are periodically made to this book as and when needed. Where appropriate and/or necessary, you must consult a professional (including but not limited to your doctor, attorney, financial advisor or such other professional advisor) before using any of the suggested remedies, techniques, or information in this book.

Upon using the contents and information contained in this book, you agree to hold harmless the Author from and against any damages, costs, and expenses, including any legal fees potentially resulting from the application of any of the information provided by this book. This disclaimer applies to any loss, damages or injury caused by the use and application, whether directly or indirectly, of any advice or information presented, whether for breach of contract, tort, negligence, personal injury, criminal intent, or under any other cause of action.

You agree to accept all risks of using the information presented in this book.

You agree that by continuing to read this book, where appropriate and/or necessary, you shall consult a professional (including but not limited to your doctor, attorney, or financial advisor or such other advisor as needed) before using any of the suggested remedies, techniques, or information in this book.

Table of Contents

1. Introduction

Perl is a general purpose high level multi-paradigm programming language. In 1987, a computer programmer named ***Larry Wall*** began working on the development of Perl language at a company called ***Unisys*** and released the first version (version 1.0) on ***December 18, 1987***. Perl is actually a set of two programming languages – ***Perl 5*** and ***Perl 6***. When we say just "***Perl***", we refer to ***Perl 5***. In October 2019, ***Perl 6*** was officially renamed to ***Raku***. In this book, we well only focus on ***Perl 5*** and refer to it as ***"Perl"***. Although ***"Perl"*** does not stand for anything, there exist many unofficial acronyms including ***"Practical Extraction and Reporting Language"***.

Perl is a cross-platform interpreted language that works on over 100 platforms. Being an interpreted language, there is a Perl interpreter that sits on the host system which executes Perl programs/scripts. Some of the well-known Perl supported platforms are ***Windows, Linux, FreeBSD, MacOS, OpenVMS, Solaris, etc.*** It is possible to write a Perl program on one platform (say Windows) and take it to another platform such as Linux or Mac and execute it. The execution will go ahead seamlessly as Perl is a cross platform language. One exception to this feature is that your program should not contain any platform specific code. In case of programming languages such as C/C++ and Java, there is a compiler which compiles a program and generates executable code. Perl adopts a different approach when it comes to program execution – being an interpreted language, a Perl script is executed line by line by the Perl interpreter.

C programming language is used to implement Perl environment. However, no knowledge of C is needed to learn Perl. Tools and languages such as ***AWK, BASIC, C/C++, sed, etc.*** have influenced Perl and languages such as ***JavaScript, CoffeeScript, Python, Ruby, PHP, etc.*** have been influenced by Perl.

2. Scope of Perl

Perl is a general purpose scripting language and can be used for many things. You can build desktop applications, web applications, web services, GUI applications, etc. with it. There are powerful set of tools for text processing, file handling, regular expression and many more. These features led to Perl's exponential growth and popularity in the 1990s and early 2000s. In 2020, Perl does not remain as popular as it used to be back in the day but is still a formidable language that can do a lot of things. In addition to the mentioned uses, Perl can be used to build network programming applications, scientific computing, system administration, etc. In fact, on Unix-like systems such as Linux, Mac and FreeBSD, system administrators use Perl to automate many tasks. Because of its power, flexibility and such diverse application space, Perl earned the nickname – ***"the Swiss Army chainsaw of scripting languages"***.

Another reason why Perl became so popular is because it emerged as the top choice for ***CGI (Common Gateway Interface) scripting***. CGI is a web server interface between the end user and non-native web application. For example, a user can interact with a Perl script using a simple webpage with the help of CGI. All this cocktail of useful features, wide use cases, power and inelegance led to this language being referred to as – ***"duct tape that hold the internet together"***.

Database management is another powerful application of Perl. Databases such as MySQL, MSSQL, PostgreSQL, MongoDB, NoSQL, SQLite, etc. can be accessed and managed using Perl with the help of appropriate APIs.

How relevant is Perl in 2020 and beyond?

Since Perl is a general purpose, cross platform scripting language, it can be used to build applications and solve problems across many domains and platforms. ***Amazon*** uses Perl for most of its backend. There is a Perl based web framework called ***catalyst*** which powers ***DuckDuckGo*** search engine's community edition and ***BBC iPlayer's*** backend. Apart from catalyst, there are some more web frameworks such as ***Mojolicious***, ***Perl Dancer***, etc. which power thousands of websites, web applications and web services. A well-known SPAM filter called ***SpamAssasin*** is written in Perl. For developing GUI applications, there are bindings available of several cross platform GUI frameworks such as ***PerlQt (for Qt), PerlTk (for Tk), wxPer (for wxWidgets), etc.***

What are the prerequisites of learning Perl?

If you already know programming languages such as C/C++, Python, Java, C#, etc. it will help you a great deal in learning Perl. If you do not, there is no need to worry as Perl is an easy to understand programming language. However, you should be comfortable with using your system and be well versed with using ***Shell/Terminal*** on Linux/MAC and ***Command Prompt/PowerShell*** on Windows.

What will I learn from this book?

Once you have gone through the whole book, you will be able to write simple command line based desktop applications that can do various things. This will set the base for learning advanced concepts. Perl is an incredibly powerful language for developing web applications. Learning web programming using Perl is pointless without understanding core web development technologies such as HTML5, CSS, JavaScript and hence web application development using Perl has not been covered in this book.

3. Getting Started

A PC/Laptop with Windows/Linux or a MAC system is needed to write and execute Perl scripts/programs. Perl programs can be written using any text editor including Notepad, Wordpad, vi, etc. I suggest ***Notepad++*** (https://notepad-plus-plus.org/). Simple Perl scripts are plain-text files and carry the extension ***.pl.*** Other extensions of Perl file types are – ***.pm, .xs, .t, .pod.*** We will only be working with the ***.pl*** file type.

As mentioned earlier, a Perl interpreter is responsible for executing Perl scripts. In this chapter, we will learn how to install Perl Interpreter.

3.1 Installing Perl on Windows

There are two major Perl implementations for Windows – ***ActiveState Perl*** and ***Strawberry Perl.*** Both implementations are official and using either one is fine for a beginner. We will be using ***Strawberry Perl*** to work with Perl scripts through the course of this book. You can choose to go ahead with ***ActiveState Perl*** should you so desire. Log on to https://www.perl.org/get.html and download the Perl interpreter of your choice. Here is how you set up ***Strawberry Perl*** on your Windows system:

Execute the installation binary. You will need Administrator rights to do so. You will be greeted with a welcome screen that looks like this:

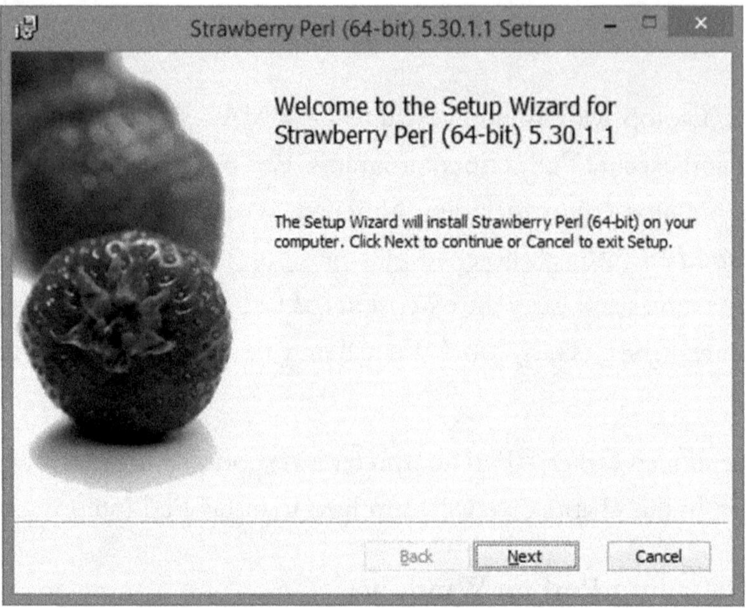

Click Next, you will be presented with the EULA:

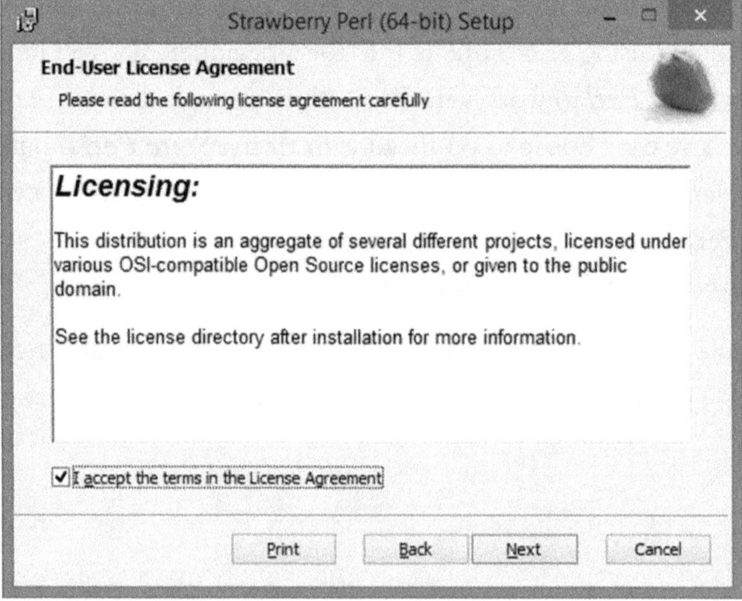

Read the agreement, accept the terms and click Next. Here, you will be given an option to choose the installation directory. It is best to leave this unchanged unless you are an advanced user and you know what you are doing.

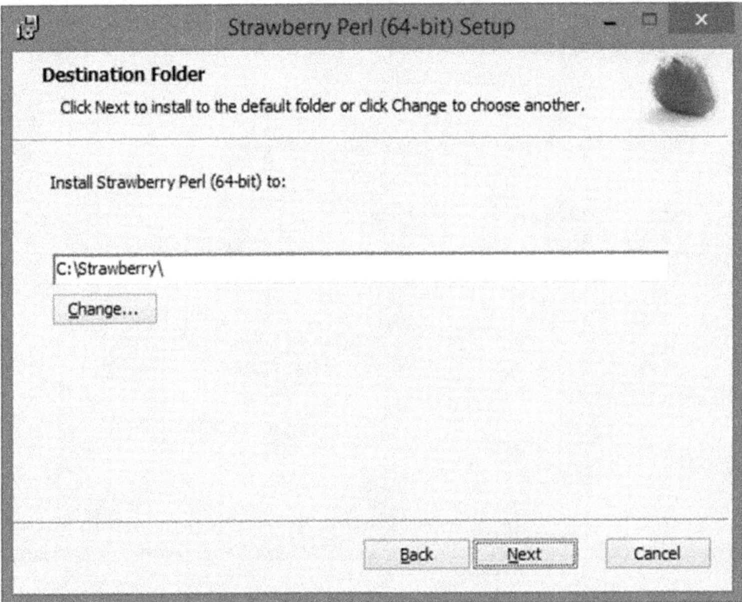

Click Install in the next Window.

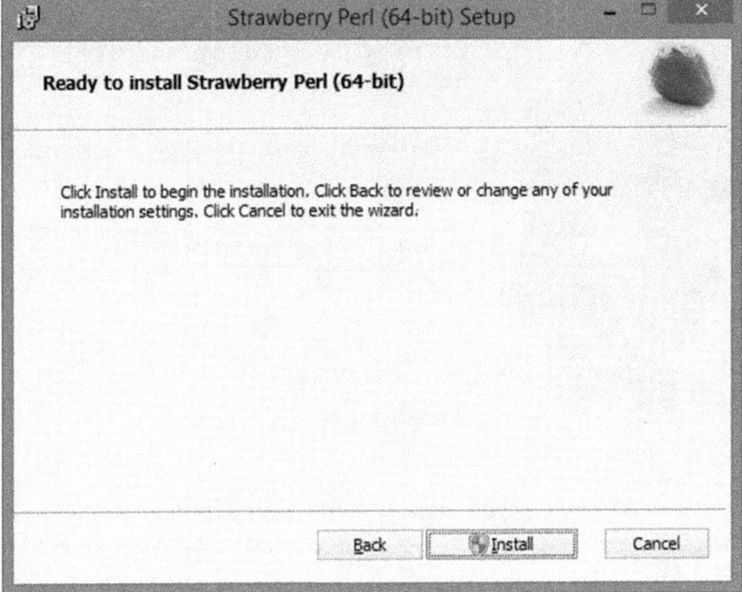

The setup process will now begin and will take a few minutes.

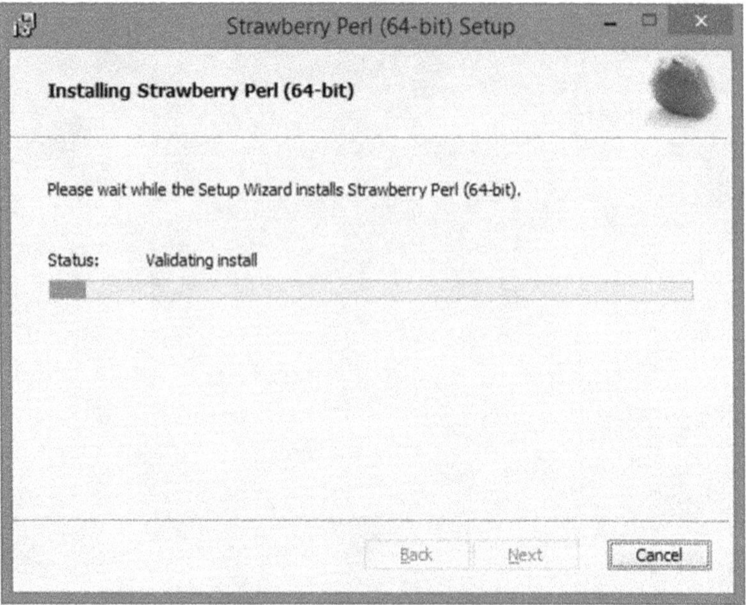

Once the installation is complete, you will see something like this:

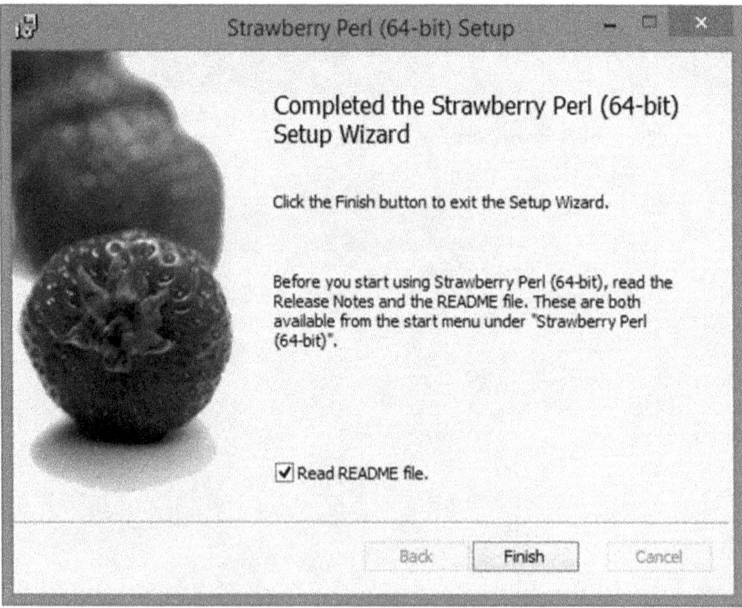

Now, open ***Command Prompt/PowerShell***, type ***perl -v*** and hit ***Enter***.

You should see Perl's version and some more information like this:

```
C:\Windows\system32\cmd.exe

F:\>perl -v

This is perl 5, version 30, subversion 1 (v5.30.1) built for MSWin32-x64-multi-t
hread

Copyright 1987-2019, Larry Wall

Perl may be copied only under the terms of either the Artistic License or the
GNU General Public License, which may be found in the Perl 5 source kit.

Complete documentation for Perl, including FAQ lists, should be found on
this system using "man perl" or "perldoc perl".  If you have access to the
Internet, point your browser at http://www.perl.org/, the Perl Home Page.

F:\>
```

If you see an error message like – ***"perl" is not recognized as an internal or external command, operable program or batch file***, it means either Perl has not been properly installed or the ***PATH*** variable has not been properly set. In such a case, make sure that ***Strawberry Perl*** has been installed by going to the installation directory (***C:\Strawberry*** in case you did not change it during installation process). Navigate to ***<drive>:\Strawberry\Perl\bin*** directory, make sure there is an executable called ***perl.exe***. If it does not exist, re-install Strawberry Perl. If it does exist, add ***<drive>:\Strawberry\Perl\bin*** to your environment variable ***PATH*** by going to ***System Properties***.

3.2 Installing Perl on Unix-like systems

If you use a Unix-like system such as Linux, MAC, FreeBSD, etc., it is likely that Perl environment is already present on your system. The best way to check is – open the Shell/Terminal and enter the following command at the prompt:

$>perl -v

This command will display Perl's version if it is present and you should see something like this:

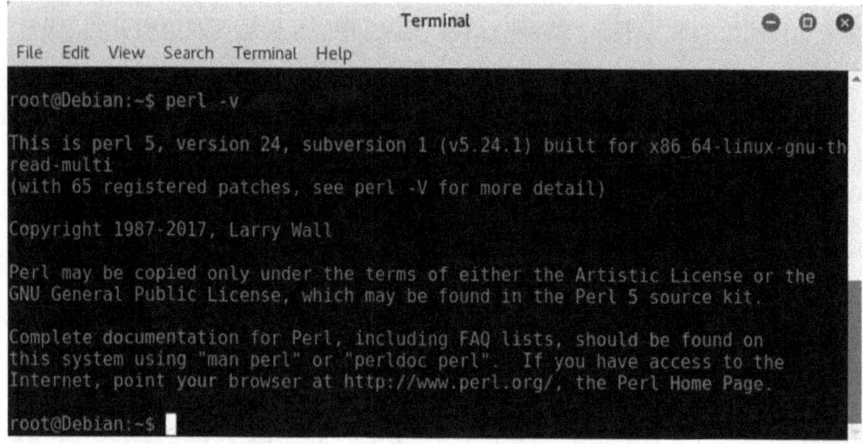

If Perl is not present, you will see an error message. In such a case, go to https://www.perl.org/get.html, download and install the appropriate version of Perl for your operating system.

3.3 Perl Scripts/Programs

A Perl script is a plain-text file containing instructions which can be written using any text editor or a supported IDE. To keep things simple, I prefer using ***Notepad++***. A script once written should be saved with the extension ***.pl***. This file is referred to as – Perl script, Perl program, Perl source, source code, source file or simply script/ program/source.

Writing Perl scripts on Windows is straight forward. Just open your favourite text editor, start writing the script and save it as ***<file name>.pl***. On Unix-like systems such as Linux, MAC, FreeBSD, etc., you have to one extra thing – add a ***shebang line***. A shebang line is a sequence of characters beginning with ***#!*** followed by the location of the environment or the script interpreter. In our case, it is the Perl interpreter. This line should be the first one in your script. The Perl interpreter is usually located at ***/usr/bin/perl*** or ***/usr/local/perl***. Hence, on Unix-like systems, the shebang line will look like:

#!/usr/bin/perl

#OR

#!/usr/local/perl

A good way to determine the location of the Perl interpreter is to use the ***where*** or ***locate*** command on Linux as follows:

$>where perl

OR

$>locate perl

On MAC, you can use the ***which*** command:

$>which perl

These commands will return the location of the Perl interpreter, simply copy it and use it as a part of your shebang like.

Note: A shebang line is not always required but is considered as a good programming practice. Hence, I suggest you always insert this line in your Perl scripts on Linux/MAC. We will look at a condition where the shebang is always required later in this chapter.

3.4 Script Execution

A Perl script can be executed on Windows and Unix-like systems by invoking the Perl interpreter using the ***perl*** command inside the Command Prompt/Powershell or Terminal/Shell. When we say ***perl*** command, it refers to the Perl interpreter's executable binary which is ***perl.exe*** on ***Windows*** (present at Perl's installation directory, eg. C:\Strawberry\perl\bin\perl.exe) and ***/usr/bin/perl*** or any other appropriate location of the Perl interpreter on Unix-like systems. The script to be executed should be passed as a command line argument to this command as follows using Command Prompt/Powershell or Terminal/Shell:

perl <script name>

Example:

perl myscript.pl

In the above example, the Perl interpreter will start executing ***myscript.pl*** Perl script. It goes without saying that the script to be executed should be present in the current working directory. Alternatively, you can provide the complete path of the script file.

There is another method of executing scripts on Unix-like systems. That is by making the script itself executable. In Linux, MAC, FreeBSD, etc. there are 3 file permissions – ***read, write and execute***. This is a vast topic and covering it is beyond the scope of this book. What we are interested in is the ***execute*** permission. A script can be made executable by giving it the execute permission. To do so, we have to use the ***chmod*** command.

In order to give execute permission to a file, we use the ***+x*** flag with the ***chmod*** command. General Syntax:

chmod +x <file 1>, <file 2>, … , <file n>

Example:

chmod +x demo.pl

chmod +x myscript.pl, yourscript.pl, ourscript.pl

Once this permission has been given to a script, it can be executed as:

./<script name>

Example:

./myscript.pl

Note: When a script is made executable, *it is mandatory to have a shebang line pointing to the environment or the location of the Perl interpreter*. Without this line, the script will not execute as it will not know which interpreter to invoke in order to begin script execution.

3.5 Hello World!!! Script Execution

Let us get hands-on experience in executing a Perl script. Open the text editor of your choice, copy-paste the following code and save it as ***helloworld.pl*** at a convenient location:

```
#This is a simple Hello World Perl Script.
#Uses print function to display text on the console.

print ("\nHello World!!!\n\n");
```

Side Note: You do not have to understand the code for now, we are only learning how to execute a script.

Let us execute this script first on Windows and then move to Unix-like systems. Open ***Command Prompt/PowerShell***, navigate using the ***cd*** command to the directory where ***helloworld.pl*** has been saved. Enter the following command:

perl helloworld.pl

You should see the output as follows:

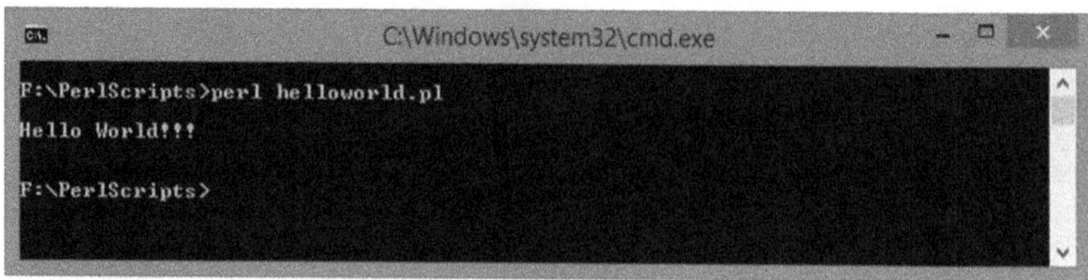

If you use Unix-like systems, modify the above code by adding the shebang line pointing to the Perl interpreter. For demonstration purpose, I am using ***Debian Linux*** and this is what my code looks like:

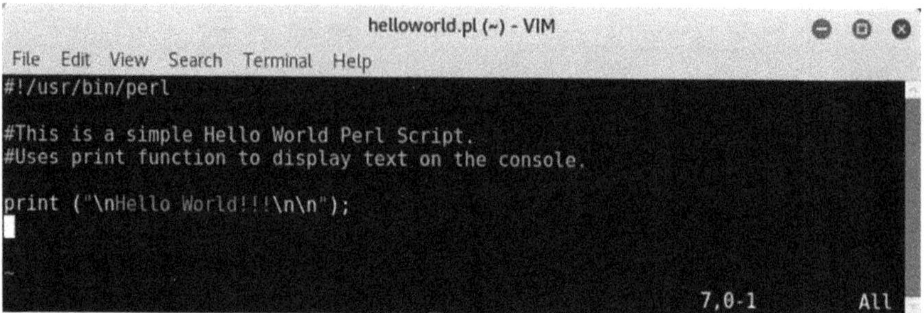

This script can be executed on Unix-like systems in two ways – by invoking the Perl interpreter and by making the script itself executable. Let us look at the Perl interpreter invocation first. Open Shell/Terminal, navigate to the directory where ***helloworld.pl*** has been saved and enter the following command:

perl helloworld.pl

You should see something like this:

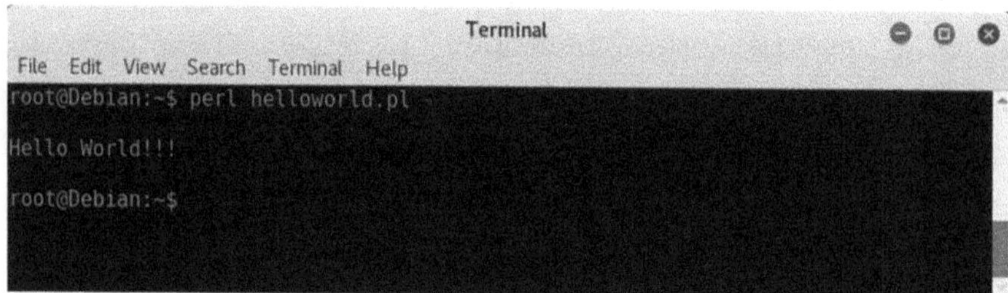

As seen this method is the same as script execution on Windows.

Let us now look at the other method where we will make this script executable using the ***chmod*** command. Open Shell/Terminal, navigate to the directory where ***helloworld.pl*** has been saved and enter the following command:

chmod +x helloworld.pl

The above command will add execute permission to ***helloworld.pl***. Enter the following command to execute the script:

./helloworld.pl

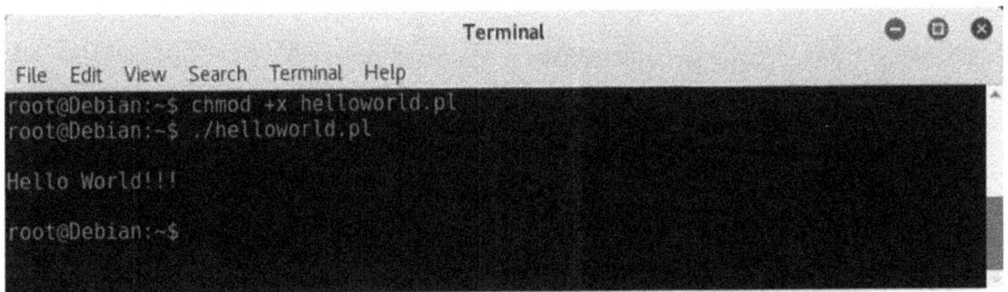

Note: The script execution process on Window and on Unix-like systems remain mostly the same. As a beginner, it does not matter which OS/Text Editor/IDEs/Tools you use to learn Perl, it is advisable to use the tools you are most comfortable with. The scripts demonstrated in the book have been written and executed on Windows and hence they do not contain shebang lines. Should you choose to execute these scripts on Unix-like systems, make sure to add the shebang line pointing to the correct location of the Perl interpreter.

4. Basic Syntax

One of the most important things about Perl you have to understand when learning it is – Perl is a case-sensitive language. Which means, "Laptop" and "laptop" are two different things to the Perl interpreter although they mean the same to us humans.

4.1 Statements

A statement is an instruction or a set of instructions that carries out a certain task or a set of tasks. A task can be anything from printing something on the console, opening/closing a file, adding two numbers, comparing two variables, etc. A statement ends with a ***semi-colon (;)***. Although you can have as many statements as you want on one line, separating each one with a semi-colon, it is a good practice to have one statement on one line. Here are a few examples of Perl statements:

print ("Hello!!!");

$number = 5 ;

*$x = 7 * 10.6 ;*

$y = $number + $x ;

4.2 Comments

Comments are usually used to mark or explain the code and are ignored by the interpreter. That is, having comments in your code will have no impact on its output. Perl supports single line comments as well as multi-line comments. A single line comment begins with a ***hash (#) symbol*** and ends on the same line. For example:

#This is a comment.

 # This is also a comment.

A multiline comment starts with an ***equal-to sign (=)*** and ends with this character sequence ***=cut***. When a multiline comment begins, the ***equal-to sign (=)*** should be immediately followed by an arbitrary character without leaving any space between the equal-to sign and the character. For example:

```
=Multiline comment begins here

Spans over many lines.

On this line too.

=cut
```

Note: Many programming examples have been demonstrated in this book. Each script is explained with comments wherever possible. It is advisable that you read through the comments for better understanding of a program.

4.3 Code Block

A code block is a group of statements. The beginning of a code block is marked with an ***open curly bracket ({)*** and the end is marked with a ***close curly bracket (})***. Close blocks are very common when dealing with decision making constructs, loops and sub-routines. For example:

```
sub DemoSub

{

        print ("This is a code block!");

}
```

4.4 Identifiers

An identifier is a name given to a variable, class, object or a sub-routine. It starts with ***$, @ or %***. An identifier name can contain alphanumeric characters and underscores. No other characters are permitted.

5. Writing your first Perl script

All the Perl scripts demonstrated in this book are essentially console applications. That is, the scripts are designed to run inside ***Command Prompt/Powershell*** or ***Shell/Terminal*** depending on the OS that you choose. In ***Section 3.5***, we saw how to execute a Perl script, in this section we will learn how to write a script to display text on the console.

5.1 print Function

One of the simplest ways to display text on the console is by using the ***print*** function. A function is reusable code designed to carry out an operation. We will be learning more about functions in depth in the ***Sub-Routines*** chapter later on, let us simply learn to use the ***print*** function for now. The print function can be used to display a constant string, variable, etc. To keep things simple, we will start with how to use print function to display a string; other features of this function will be covered as and when required. A string is a sequence of characters enclosed within ***double quotes (" ")***.

The general syntax of print function to display a string is:

print (<string>);

#OR

print <string>;

Example:

print ("This should work!");

print "This is another example.";

Let us write a simple Perl script with one print statement to display text on the console. Open a text editor, write a ***print*** statement to display the string of your choice, save the file using ***.pl*** extension. Run the script using the ***perl*** command. Here is my script:

```
#This is the first program we're actually writing.
print ("This is my first Perl script!");
```

<u>Output:</u>

```
Command Prompt
F:\PerlScripts>perl firstprogram.pl
This is my first Perl script!
F:\PerlScripts>
```

Let us now insert one more print statement to print another string after the first one and see what happens:

```
#This is the first program we're actually writing.
print ("This is my first Perl script!");
print ("Wow!!! This works!");
```

<u>Output:</u>

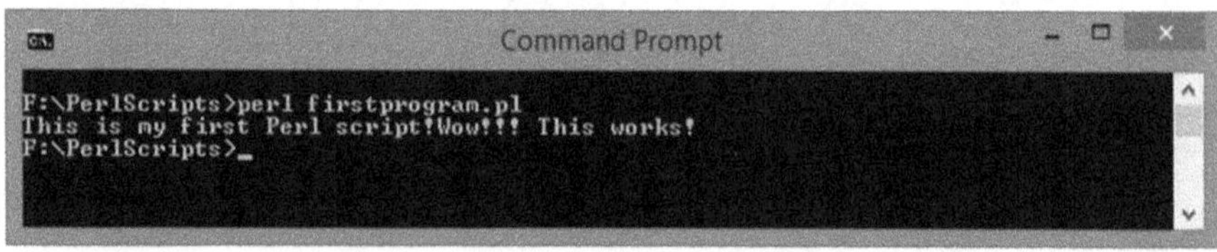

Notice how the second string is printed on the same line as the first one. In fact, not even a space has been left between the end of the first line and the beginning of the second one. If we leave space at the end of the first line, it will obviously reflect in the output. Modify the first print statement to the following and verify the output:

```
print ("This is my first Perl script! ");
```

Output:

Text can be printed on the next line by using the escape character sequence ***\n***. Another useful one is ***\t*** which is used to inset a tab-space. Here is an example:

```
#Escape Character Demo
print ("\nLet us see how to print on the next line.");
print ("\nThis is how you do it.");
print ("\nAnd \tthis is how \tyou leave a \ttab-
space.\n")
```

Output:

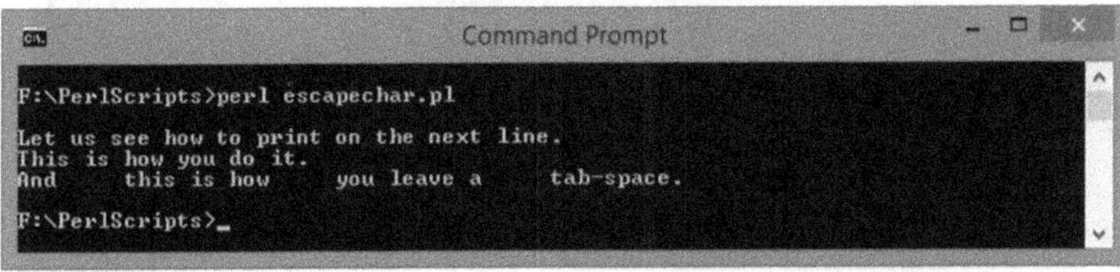

Note: Backslash (\) is the character used to escape characters such as restricted ones' like ***@, $*** and ***%***. For example, if you want to display ***$*** using a ***print*** statement, you cannot do it directly because ***$*** means something else in Perl (we will cover it later). This is where the escape character backslash is very useful. Instead of saying:

print ("$");

You would say:

print ("\$");

5.2 Syntax Errors

Syntax errors will be encountered when proper syntax has not been followed. When you try to run a script containing syntax errors, sometimes the interpreter will point out exactly where what has gone wrong and sometimes the error description will be vague. Hence, it is advisable that you follow the correct syntax and check your code thoroughly before running. Let us take an example of a code with syntax errors:

```
print ("Forgetting semi colon on purpose.")
print ("\nLets see what happens.")
```

I have omitted semi-colons at the end of print statements on purpose. When you try to run this code, this is what you should see:

```
Command Prompt
F:\PerlScripts>perl test.pl
syntax error at test.pl line 2, near ")
print"
Execution of test.pl aborted due to compilation errors.

F:\PerlScripts>
```

This error message gives you a fair idea of what is wrong with your code.

6. Data Types and Variables

A ***data type*** is used to understand the category of data we are working with. A ***variable*** is a name given to a memory location. Perl offers three basic data types – ***scalar, arrays and hashes***.

6.1 Data Types

Let us take a look at each of these 3 categories very briefly.

6.1.1 Scalar

Scalar variables are used to store numbers and strings. Numbers can be integers, floating point values, hexadecimal and octal. Scalar variable names begin with a ***dollar sign ($)***.

6.1.2 Arrays

An array is a collection of items. Array variables begin with ***at the rate sign (@)***.

6.1.3 Hashes

Hashes are used to store data using key-value pairs. Hash variables begin with ***percentage sign (%)***.

6.2 Variables

A variable is an identifier used to address a memory location. When a variable is declared, some amount of memory is reserved for it to store its contents. This memory location can be uniquely addressed using its memory address. Because it would be difficult for programmers to remember memory location every time they access data from a memory location, there is a concept of variables. In this section, we will only talk about ***Scalar Variables.*** There are dedicated chapters on ***Arrays*** and ***Hashes*** later in this book.

6.2.1 Declaring Scalar Variables

A scalar variable name begins with a ***dollar sign ($)***, can contain alphanumeric characters and underscores. The first character has to be either an alphabet or an underscore. Assignment operator given by the ***equal-to sign (=)*** is used to assign values to variables. A variable can be declared and initialized in the simplest way using the following syntax:

```
$<variable name> = <initial value>;
```

Example:

```
$name = "Rose";

$age = 29;

$weight = 45.74;
```

6.2.2 Numeric Values

Integers, floats, octal, hexadecimal and scientific notations are supported by Perl as numbers in general. Here are a few examples:

```
#Integers

$num1 = 9;

$num2 = 27;

#Floating point values

$x = 5.86;

$y = -66.356;

#Octal (Begins with 0)
```

$m = 0464;

$n = -033;

#Hexadecimal

$hex_1 = 0xFA;

$hex_2 = 0xceb;

#Scientific Notations (Used for large floating point values)

$r = -3.5E6;

$s = 8.65E-2;

6.2.3 String Values

A string can be formed by enclosing a sequence of characters either in ***single-quotes*** or ***double-quotes*** but not in a mixed order. Here are a few examples:

$name = "Yuan";

$address = 'Xiamen';

If you want to include a restricted character such as ***$, %, @,*** etc. you have to use the ***escape character (\)*** just before the restricted character. For example, if you want to store an email address in a string variable you cannot do it directly as the ***@ sign*** will cause problems. Instead of the following statement:

#This statement is wrong, used only for demonstration purpose

$email = "user@xyzdomain.com"

You will have to use the escape character as follows:

```
$email = "user\@xyzdomain.com"
```

6.2.4 Display Scalar Variables

The contents of scalar variables can be displayed using the ***print*** function. It is possible to display a single variable, multiple variables separated by commas or make multiple variables part of one big string. Consider the following code snippet, all the ***print*** statements are syntactically valid:

```
$name = "Jody";
$company = "Microsoft";
$package = 120;
#Display single variable
print ($name);
#Display multiple variables, separated by comma.
#No space will be left when these variable will be printed.
print ($name, $company, package);
#Display multiple variables, separated by comma.
#Insert space between variables.
print ($name, " ", $company, " ", package);
#Make variables part of a larger string
print ("\nName: $name \nCompany = $company \nPackage =
$package \n");
```

Let us write a Perl script to demonstrate the usage of variables:

```
#Variables Demo
#Declare and initialize different types of numbers
#Integer
$x = 25;
#Float
$y = -54.7098;
#Scientific Notation
$z = 1.397E-2;
#Hexadecimal
$h1 = 0x4a6b;
$h2 = -0x3c;
#Octal
$oct = 0345;
#Display everything
print ("\nx = $x \t\ty = $y \tz = $z \nh1 = $h1 \th2 =
$h2 \toct = $oct\n\n");

#Declare and initialize strings
$name = 'Maggie';
$country = "South Africa";
$email = "maggie\@somedomainxyz.com";
#Print everything
print ("\nname: $name \ncountry: $country \nemail:
$email \n\n");
```

Output:

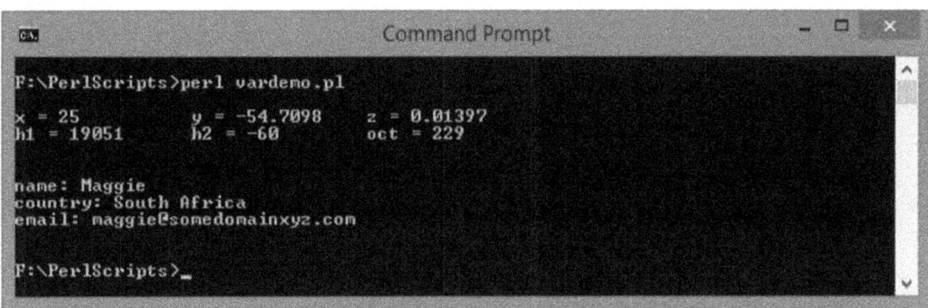

Suggestion: Whenever you use variables to store any data, always use meaningful variable names. For example, if you want to store salary of a person, you would be better off using a variable name such as ***$salary*** or ***$sal*** as compared to ***$x, $y, etc***. This is not only considered a good programming practice but will also make your code readable and easy to understand.

7. User Interaction

Whatever scripts we have seen so far, did not involve any input from the user. A user simply had to execute them. In this section, we will see how to accept input from the user. There are various input/output devices (I/O) connected to a computer. The standard output device is the monitor in most cases and the standard input device is the keyboard in most cases. It takes a lot of things internally for such devices to be interfaced with a computer and deal with input and output. But for an end user, there is nothing much to worry about as these things happen implicitly. The standard input and output devices are abbreviated as ***STDIN*** and ***STDIO*** respectively.

In order to accept input from a user, we use the ***Prompt***, given by ***<STDIN>*** or simply ***<>***. A scalar variable is needed to receive the input coming from the user. General Syntax:

$[Scalar Variable] = <>;

#OR

$[Scalar Variable] = <STDIN>;

Example:

$name = <>;

#OR

$address = <STDIN>;

When a prompt is used, it will introduce a ***blocking I/O operation*** into your program. That is, whenever the interpreter encounters a statement containing ***<>*** or ***<STDIN>***, the program will halt and wait for the user to enter something through the keyboard (and press ***Enter***). No other I/O interaction will happen with the program until the user gives some input. When the user enters something and presses ***Enter***, that data will be stored in the variable specified on the left hand side. If the user does not enter anything at all, the script will wait at that point indefinitely until the process is terminated externally.

Let us write a Perl script which will ask the user to enter a message and the same message will be displayed back.

```
#User Input Demo 1
#Ask the user to enter something
print ("\nEnter some text: ");
#Use prompt to receive the input in the variable $message
$message = <STDIN>;
#Display the contents of $message
print ("\nYou have entered: $message");
```

Output:

```
Command Prompt
F:\PerlScripts>perl displaymsg.pl
Enter some text: This is just some random text!
You have entered: This is just some random text!
F:\PerlScripts>_
```

This is a critical chapter as it introduces user interaction during runtime for the first time in this book. Let us take another example where we shall ask the user to enter name, age, address and country. We will then display the entered data. Here is the script:

```
#User Input Demo 2
#Ask the user to enter name
print ("\nEnter your name: ");
#Use prompt to receive the input in the variable $name
$name = <STDIN>;
#Ask the user to enter age
print ("\nEnter your age: ");
#Use prompt to receive the input in the variable $age
$age = (<STDIN>);
#Ask the user to enter address
```

```
print ("\nEnter your address: ");
#Use prompt to receive the input in the variable $address
$address = <STDIN>;
#Ask the user to enter country
print ("\nEnter your country: ");
#Use prompt to receive the input in the variable $country
$country = <STDIN>;
#Display Everything
print ("\nYou have entered: \n\nname:\t\t$name
\nage:\t\t$age \naddress:\t$address
\ncountry:\t$country ");
```

Output:

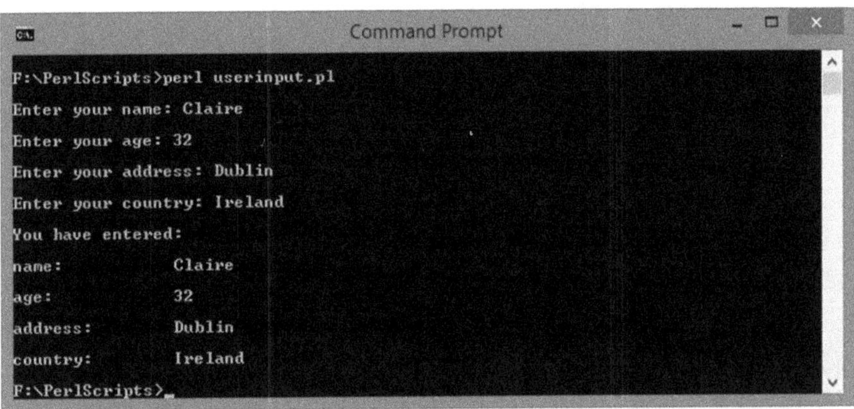

```
F:\PerlScripts>perl userinput.pl
Enter your name: Claire
Enter your age: 32
Enter your address: Dublin
Enter your country: Ireland
You have entered:
name:           Claire
age:            32
address:        Dublin
country:        Ireland
F:\PerlScripts>_
```

When we enter something through the keyboard and press ***Enter***, ***newline character (\n)*** is appended to our input. Take a look at the print statement from the previous example:

```
print ("\nYou have entered: \n\nname:\t\t$name
\nage:\t\t$age \naddress:\t$address
\ncountry:\t$country ");
```

Except for ***\n\nname***, there is only one ***\n*** each in front of ***age***, ***address*** and ***country***. Yet, one extra line is left when we try to print the contents of the variables. This is because, the newline character that got appended to our input whenever we entered something and pressed Enter is leaving one extra line. To circumvent this, we can use the ***chomp*** function which will remove the trailing newline character. It can be used either while taking the input with prompt ***(<> / <STDIN>)*** or once the input is received into a variable, ***chomp*** function can be used on that variable. General syntax:

chomp ($[scalar variable] = <STDIN>);

#OR

$[scalar variable] = <STDIN>);

chomp ($[scalar variable]);

Example:

chomp ($name = <>);

#OR

$name = <>;

chomp ($name);

Let us modify the above code to demonstrate both ways of using chomp function:

```
#User Input Demo 2
#Ask the user to enter name
print ("\nEnter your name: ");
#Use prompt to receive the input in the variable $name
#Use chomp at the time of taking input.
chomp ($name = <STDIN>);
#Ask the user to enter age
print ("\nEnter your age: ");
#Use prompt to receive the input in the variable $age
#Use chomp at the time of taking input.
chomp ($age = (<>));
#Ask the user to enter address
print ("\nEnter your address: ");
#Use prompt to receive the input in the variable $address
$address = <STDIN>;
#Use chomp after taking the input
chomp ($address);
#Ask the user to enter country
print ("\nEnter your country: ");
```

```
#Use prompt to receive the input in the variable $country
$country = <>;
#Use chomp after taking the input
chomp ($country);
#Display Everything
print ("\nAfter running your input through chomp
function: \n\nname:\t\t$name \nage:\t\t$age
\naddress:\t$address \ncountry:\t$country ");
```

<u>Output:</u>

```
Command Prompt
F:\PerlScripts>perl userinput.pl
Enter your name: Earl
Enter your age: 43
Enter your address: Austin
Enter your country: USA
After running your input through chomp function:
name:           Earl
age:            43
address:        Austin
country:        USA
F:\PerlScripts>_
```

As seen, an extra line has not been left after the input has been run through the ***chomp*** function. The usage of chomp function is not mandatory every time user input is received but is advisable. This is because, the trailing newline character can make your code unstable in certain situations.

Note: Whenever an input is received via the prompt, its datatype is determined implicitly. For example, if a user enters alphanumeric characters, it will be treated as a string. If you enter any form of number be it integer, float, scientific notation, hexadecimal or octal, it will be treated as a number. <u>Whenever, you are dealing with numbers, it is highly recommended that you use the chomp function either while taking the input or soon after</u>.

8. Operators

An operator is a symbol or a group of symbols used to carry out an operation such as arithmetic operation, logical operation, assignment operation, etc. Perl offers arithmetic operators, assignment operators, comparison operators, logical operators and bitwise operators. We will take a look at each of these categories of operators along with programming examples at the end of each section.

8.1 Arithmetic Operators

These operators are used to carry out arithmetic operations such as addition, subtraction, multiplication, division, etc.

Operator	Description	Sample Usage	Explanation
+	Addition	$a + $b	Performs addition and returns the sum of all the operands.
-	Subtraction	$a - $b	Subtracts the operand on the right from the operand on the left.
*	Multiplication	$a * $b	Multiplies operands and returns the product.
/	Division	$a / $b	Divides the operand on the left by the operand on the right and returns the quotient.
%	Modulus	$a % $b	Divides the operand on the left by the operand on the right and returns the remainder. This operator will work correctly only with integers.
**	Exponent	$a ** $b	Raises the power of the operand on the left by a value specified by the operand on the right. Eg. 5 ** 2 is equivalent to 5^2 in mathematical form which is equal to 25.
++	Increment	$a ++	Increments the value of the given variable by one. $a++ is equivalent to $a = $a + 1.
--	Decrement	$b --	Decrements the value of the given variable by one. $b-- is equivalent to $b = $b - 1.

Here is a Perl script that demonstrates the usage of arithmetic operators:

```
#Arithmetic Operators Demo
#Declare some variables
$x = 35;
$y = 3;
$z = -9.34;
#Addition Operator
$sum = $x + $y + $z;
#Subtraction Operator
$diff = $x - $z;
#Multiplication Operator
$prod = $x * $y * $z;
#Division Operator
$q = $x / $y;
#Modulus Operator
$mod = $x % $y;
#Exponent Operator
$exp = $x ** $y;
#Display Everything
print ("\nx = $x\ny = $y\nz = $z");
print ("\nx + y + z = $sum\nx - z = $diff");
print ("\nx * y * z = $prod\nx / y = $q");
print ("\nx % y = $mod\nx ** y = $exp\n");
```

<u>Output:</u>

```
Command Prompt

F:\PerlScripts>perl aithmeticoperators.pl

x = 35
y = 3
z = -9.34
x + y + z = 28.66
x - z = 44.34
x * y * z = -980.7
x / y = 11.6666666666667
x % y = 2
x ** y = 42875

F:\PerlScripts>
```

Let us now write another program where we will accept two numbers from the user and calculate their sum, difference, product and quotient. We will use the ***chomp*** function at the time of taking the input.

```
#Arithmetic Operators Demo
#Declare some variables
print ("\nEnter the value of x: ");
#Use prompt to receive the input into variable $x
#Use chomp at the time of taking input.
chomp ($x = <STDIN>);
print ("\nEnter the value of y: ");
#Use prompt to receive the input into variable $y
#Use chomp at the time of taking input.
chomp ($y = <STDIN>);
#Calculate sum
$sum = $x + $y;
#Calculate difference
$difference = $x - $y;
#Multiply
$product = $x * $y ;
#Divide
$quotient = $x / $y;
#Display Everything
print ("\nx = $x\ny = $y");
print ("\nx + y = $sum\nx - y = $difference");
print ("\nx * y = $product\nx / y = $quotient\n");
```

<u>Output:</u>

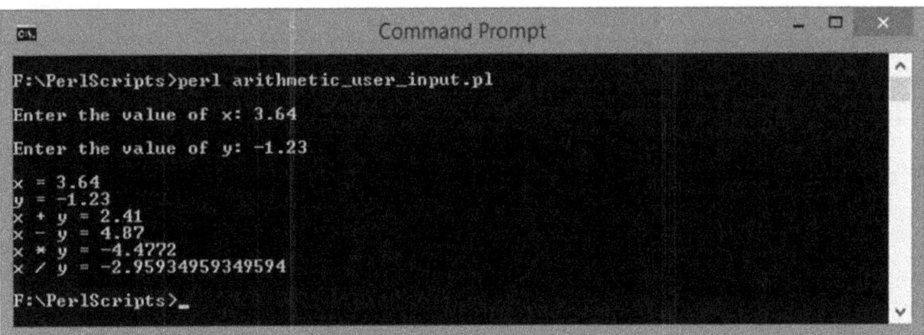

Command Prompt
F:\PerlScripts>perl arithmetic_user_input.pl
Enter the value of x: 3.64
Enter the value of y: -1.23
x = 3.64
y = -1.23
x + y = 2.41
x - y = 4.87
x * y = -4.4772
x / y = -2.95934959349594
F:\PerlScripts>

Note: You can use multiple arithmetic operators in one expression like ***$a** = 4 * 3 – 2 / 9.* In such cases, mathematical rules of evaluation will apply. That is, *2 / 9* and *4 * 3* will be performed first and then subtraction will be performed. You can also use brackets to avoid confusion. Here is an example – ***$a** = **$b** + (3 * 5.1) / (1.4 + (2 * 1.6)).*

8.2 Assignment Operators

We have seen the usage of the default assignment operator given by the ***equal-to (=)*** sign. There are more such operators which are used to assign values to variables.

Operator	Description	Sample Usage	Equivalent Expression
+=	Add operands, assign sum to the operand on the left.	$a += $b	$a = $a + $b
-=	Subtract the operand on the right from the one on the left and assign the difference to the left operand.	$a -= $b	$a = $a - $b
*=	Perform multiplication and assign the product to the operand on the left.	$a *= $b	$a = $a * $b
/=	Divide the left operand by the right one and assign the quotient to the left operand.	$a /= $b	$a = $a / $b
%=	Divide the left operand by the right one and assign the remainder to the left operand.	$a %= $b	$a = $a % $b
**=	Calculate exponent and assign the value to the left operand.	$a **= $b	$a = $a ** $b

Here is a script that demonstrate the usage of assignment operators:

```
#Assignment Operators Demo
#Initialize some variables
$a = -12;
$b = 65;
$c = 3;
$d = 5.68;
#Display all values
print ("\na = $a, b = $b, c = $c, d = $d");
# += operator
$a += $b;
print ("\n\$a += \$b = $a, a = $a, b = $b, c = $c, d =
$d");
# -= operator
$a -= $b;
```

```
print ("\n\$a -= \$b = $a, a = $a, b = $b, c = $c, d =
$d");
# *= operator
$b *= $c;
print ("\n\$b *= \$c = $b, a = $a, b = $b, c = $c, d =
$d");
# /= operator
$a /= $d;
print ("\n\$a /= \$d = $a, a = $a, b = $b, c = $c, d =
$d");
# %= operator
$b %= $c;
print ("\n\$b %= \$c = $b, a = $a, b = $b, c = $c, d =
$d");
# ^^= operator
$c **= $d;
print ("\n\$c **= \$d = $c, a = $a, b = $b, c = $c, d =
$d\n");
```

Output:

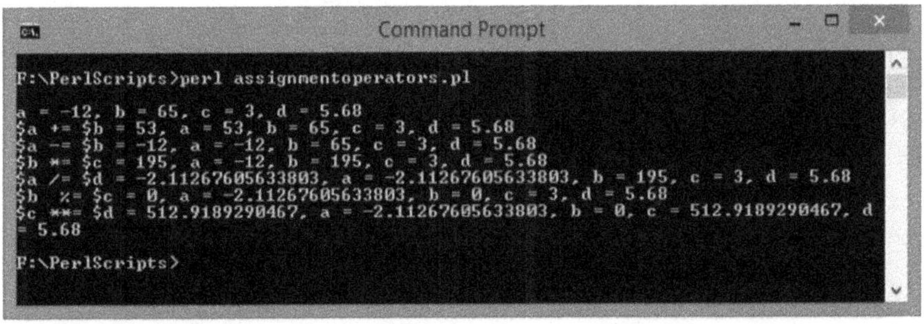

```
Command Prompt
F:\PerlScripts>perl assignmentoperators.pl

a = -12, b = 65, c = 3, d = 5.68
$a += $b = 53, a = 53, b = 65, c = 3, d = 5.68
$a -= $b = -12, a = -12, b = 65, c = 3, d = 5.68
$b *= $c = 195, a = -12, b = 195, c = 3, d = 5.68
$a /= $d = -2.11267605633803, a = -2.11267605633803, b = 195, c = 3, d = 5.68
$b  %= $c = 0, a = -2.11267605633803, b = 0, c = 3, d = 5.68
$c **= $d = 512.9189290467, a = -2.11267605633803, b = 0, c = 512.9189290467, d
= 5.68

F:\PerlScripts>
```

Note: These assignment operators will assign the value resulting from an operation to the operand on the left (which is also used in the arithmetic operation itself). This will make the left operand lose its original value and hence usage of these operators may not be suitable in every situation. In the above example, there are four variables – ***$a, $b, $c and $d***. All these variables are printed after every operation to show their changing values.

8.3 Comparison Operators

Comparison operators are used to compare one operand in relation to another. The result of these operations is either ***Boolean True*** or ***Boolean False***. We will only learn the theory behind comparison operators, their usage will be better understood in the ***Decision Making*** and ***Loops*** chapters.

Operator	Description	Sample Usage	Explanation
==	Equal To	$a == $b	Returns ***True*** if both the operands are ***equal***, ***False*** otherwise.
!=	Not Equal To	$a != $b	Returns ***True*** if both the operands are ***NOT equal***, ***False*** otherwise.
<	Less Than	$a < $b	Returns ***True*** if the value of the operand on the left ***is less than*** the value of the operand on the right, ***False*** otherwise.
>	Greater Than	$a > $b	Returns ***True*** if the value of the operand on the left ***is greater than*** the value of the operand on the right, ***False*** otherwise.
<=	Less Than OR Equal To	$a <= $b	Returns ***True*** if the value of the operand on the left ***is less than OR equal to*** the value of the operand on the right, ***False*** otherwise.
>=	Greater Than OR Equal To	$a >= $b	Returns ***True*** if the value of the operand on the left ***is greater than OR equal to*** the value of the operand on the right, ***False*** otherwise.

8.4 Logical Operators

Logical operators are used to carry out logical ***OR, AND*** and ***NOT***. Outcome of logical operations result in ***Boolean True or False*** and are usually used with expressions that result in ***Boolean True or False*** in the first place. For example, an expression could be a comparison operation such as ***$a > $b***. The usage of these operators will also be clearer when we learn ***Decision Making*** and ***Loops***.

Operator	Description	Sample Usage	Explanation
and #Alternative# &&	Logical AND	(Expr1) and (Expr2) #Alternative# (Expr1) && (Expr2)	Returns ***True*** if all the expressions evaluate to ***True***, ***False*** otherwise.
or #Alternative# ||	Logical OR	(Expr1) or (Expr2) #Alternative# (Expr1) || (Expr2)	Returns ***True*** if any one of the expressions evaluates to ***True***. Returns ***False*** if all the expressions evaluate to ***False***.
!	Logical NOT	! (Expr)	Inverts the result. If the expression evaluates to ***False***, ***True*** will be returned and if it evaluates to ***True***, ***False*** will be returned.

8.5 Bitwise Operators

Bitwise operators carry out logical operations like OR, AND, XOR and a few others on each bit of the operands. In order to understand this class of operators, you need to understand the basics of binary number system and Boolean algebra.

Operator	Description	Sample Usage	Explanation
&	Bitwise Logical AND	$a & $b	Performs logical AND on each corresponding bit of the operands.
|	Bitwise Logical OR	$a | $b	Performs logical OR on each corresponding bit of the operands.
~	Bitwise Logical Inverter	~$a	Computes binary one's compliment.
^	Bitwise Logical XOR	$a ^ $b	Performs logical XOR on each corresponding bit of the operands.
<<	Left Shift	$a << $b	Left shifts bits of the operand on the left as many times as specified by the operand on the right. Eg. 2 << 3 will left shift 2's bits (10 in binary) 3 times. So, 2 << 3 will be equal to 16 (10000 in binary)
>>	Right Shift	$a >> $b	Right shifts bits of the operand on the left as many times as specified by the operand on the right. Eg. 7 >> 1 will right shift 7's bits (111 in binary) 1 time. So, 7 >> 1 will be equal to 3 (11 in binary).

Let us write a Perl script to demonstrate the usage of Bitwise operators:

```
#Bitwise Operators Demo
#Initialize some variables
$a = 13;
$b = 11;
$c = 2;
$d = 3;
#Display all values
print ("\na = $a, b = $b, c = $c, d = $d");
#Bitwise OR
$x = $a | $b ;
#Bitwise AND
$y = $a & $b ;
#Bitwise XOR
$z = $a ^ $b ;
#Left shift
$p = $a << $c ;
#Right Shift
$q = $b >> $d ;
#Display Everything
print ("\n\na | b = $x \na & b = $y \na ^ b = $z");
print ("\na << c = $p \nb >> d = $q\n");
```

<u>Output:</u>

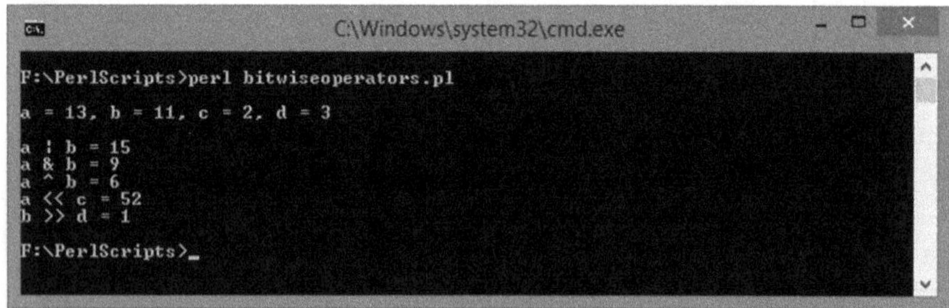

Note: There are a few more operators such as the ones used to work with strings. They will be covered in the relevant chapters.

9. Decision Making

So far, we have seen how a Perl script executes from top to bottom statement by statement. This is a normal flow of execution. If we want to alter this flow of execution and introduce conditionality, we have to make use of ***Control Structures.*** Perl offers control structures in the form of ***Decision Making*** constructs and ***Loops.*** In this chapter we will learn about the various decision making constructs and in the next chapter, we will learn about loops.

Let us take a look at the various decision making constructs available in Perl.

9.1 if-else Statements

if-else constructs are used when we want to execute a block of code when a particular condition is true. The simplest way of using this construct is to use a single ***if*** statement. Here is the general syntax:

```
if (<condition>)
{
        #Code to be executed if <condition> is true.
}
```

Example:

```
if ($x > 1)
{
        print ("$x is greater than 1");
}
```

The ***if statement*** should be supplied with a ***condition***, given by ***<condition>*** in the above code snippet. When the execution control encounters an ***if*** statement, this ***<condition>*** will be evaluated. If it evaluates to ***true***, the statements inside the ***if-block*** (enclosed within *{ }* following the ***if*** statement) will be executed. If the condition evaluates to ***false***, the if block will be skipped and the script will resume execution from the end of the ***if-block*** provided there are statements after the ***if-block***.

Note 1: The ***<condition>*** that we talked about should evaluate to Boolean ***true*** or ***false***. It is usually an expression made up of comparison operators or a group of expressions combined together with logical operators. Some of the examples of valid conditions are:

```
($a > 5)

($b == 0) && ($a > -6)

($x > 10) || ($y < 20)
```

Note 2: Number ***0*** and ***empty strings ("")*** are considered as ***false***.

With a single ***if statement***, we check for the validity of one condition; if it is valid, we execute some statements, if it is not valid, we do nothing. If we want execute a block of code when the given condition of the ***if statement*** evaluates to ***false***, we can use an ***else*** block. General syntax:

```
if (<condition>)

{

        #Code to be executed if <condition> is true.

}

else
```

{

#Code to be executed if <condition> is false.

}

Example:

if ($x > 1)

{

print ("$x is greater than 1");

}

else

{

print ("$x is NOT greater than 1");

}

When there is an ***if block*** and an ***else block***. If the given ***condition*** of the ***if block*** evaluates to ***false***, the ***if block*** will be skipped and the statements inside the ***else block*** will be executed one by one. Let us understand this with an example. We will write a script to accept one integer from the user and check if it is odd or even:

```
#If-Else demo. Check if a number is odd or even
print ("\nEnter an integer: ");
#Use prompt to receive the input into variable $num
#Use chomp at the time of taking input.
chomp ($num = <STDIN>);
#Check if the number is divisible by 2.
#If so, it is even.
if ($num % 2 == 0)
{
	print("\n$num is even.\n");
}
else
{
	print("\n$num is odd.\n");
}
```

Output:

```
Command Prompt
F:\PerlScripts>perl oddeven.pl
Enter an integer: 19
19 is odd.
F:\PerlScripts>perl oddeven.pl
Enter an integer: 32
32 is even.
F:\PerlScripts>_
```

A pair of ***if-else*** blocks will check for one condition, do something based on the validity of the given condition and do something else upon its invalidity. If you want to check for multiple conditions, you can nest if-else blocks. That is, you can place ***if-else*** blocks inside other ***if-else*** blocks where outer blocks will check for one condition, the inner ones will check for another condition. Another way of checking for multiple conditions is to use the ***elsif*** statement. The way this works is – there should be a mandatory ***if block***, then there could be multiple ***elsif block***, where each ***elsif*** statement will have its own condition. Refer to the following code snippet:

```
if ( <condition 1>)
{
        #This block will be executed if <condition 1> is true.
        #Statements…
}
elsif ( <condition 2> )
{
        #This block will be executed if <condition 1> is false
        <condition 2> is true.
```

```
        #Statements...
    }
    elsif ( <condition 3> )
    {
        #This block will be executed if <condition 1> and <condition
        2> are false and <condition 3> is true.
        #Statements...
    }
    else
    {
        #This block will be executed if <condition 1>, <condition 2>
and                         <condition 3> are false.
        #Statements...
    }
```

When the condition of an ***if statement*** evaluates to ***false***, the interpreter will look for an ***elsif*** statement. Its condition will be evaluated. If it evaluates to ***true***, the statements inside that ***elsifblock*** will be executed. If the condition evaluates to ***false***, the execution control will jump to the next ***elsif*** statement (if it is present) and its condition will be checked. This process will go on until one of the conditions (either of the only ***if statement*** or one of the ***elsif*** statements) evaluates to ***true*** or there are no more ***elsif blocks*** left. When none of the conditions evaluate to true, the ***else block*** will be executed if it is present.

Let us understand how the combination of ***if-elsif-else*** blocks work. We will write a Perl script where the user will be asked to enter a number and we will check whether the number is positive, negative or zero:

```
#If-ElsIf-Else demo. Check if a number is positive,
negative or zero
print ("\nEnter a number: ");
#Use prompt to receive the input into variable $num
#Use chomp at the time of taking input.
chomp ($num = <STDIN>);
#Check if the number is greater than 0.
#If so, it is positive
if ($num > 0)
{
      print("\n$num is positive.\n");
}
#Check if the number is less than 0.
#If so, it is positive
elsif ($num < 0)
{
      print("\n$num is negative.\n");
}
#If the number is neither positive nor negative, means
it is zero.
else
{
      print ("\n$num is zero.\n")
}
```

Output:

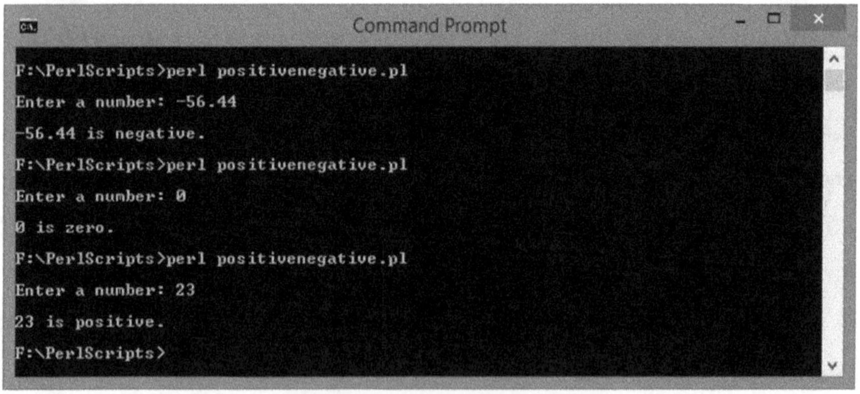

```
F:\PerlScripts>perl positivenegative.pl
Enter a number: -56.44
-56.44 is negative.
F:\PerlScripts>perl positivenegative.pl
Enter a number: 0
0 is zero.
F:\PerlScripts>perl positivenegative.pl
Enter a number: 23
23 is positive.
F:\PerlScripts>
```

Notes:

1. An ***if-block*** can be standalone while ***elsif*** and ***else*** blocks cannot. They need a preceding ***if-block*** in order to work.
2. ***if*** and ***elsif*** statements should be supplied with a condition while ***else*** statement should not be.
3. Other than ***elsif*** blocks, there should be no other statements sandwiched between an ***if block*** and an ***else block***.
4. When an ***if block*** is followed by multiple ***elsif*** blocks, ***ONLY ONE*** of these blocks will be executed when a corresponding valid condition is found. Rest of the blocks will be skipped. As the execution control will proceed sequentially, even if there is an ***elsif*** block with a valid condition somewhere further down, it will be skipped if one of the blocks before this block gets executed.

9.2 unless Statement

Contrary to the ***if*** statement, the ***unless statement*** is used to execute a block of code when a condition is ***NOT true***. This construct also needs to be supplied with a condition. Here is the general syntax:

```
unless (<condition>)
{
        #Statements to be executed if <condition> is NOT true.
}
```

Example:

```
unless ($a == 0)
{
        print ("a is Non-Zero");
}
```

The ***unless block*** can be followed by an ***else block*** which will be executed if the ***<condition>*** of the ***unless statement*** evaluates to ***true***. In comparison to the ***if-else*** combination, the ***unless-else*** combination does the exact opposite. Here is how to use the ***unless-else*** combination:

```
unless (<condition>)
{
    #Statements to be executed if <condition> is NOT true.
}
else
{
    #Statements to be executed if <condition> is true.
}
```

Example:

```
unless ($a == 0)
{
    print ("a is Non-Zero");
}
else
{
    print ("a is Zero");
}
```

Let us re-write the odd-even script using unless-else blocks:

```
#Unless-Else demo. Check if a number is odd or even
print ("\nEnter an integer: ");
#Use prompt to receive the input into variable $num
#Use chomp at the time of taking input.
chomp ($num = <STDIN>);
#Check if the number is not divisible by 2.
#If so, it is odd.
unless ($num % 2 == 0)
{
	print("\n$num is odd.\n");
}
#Otherwise it is even.
else
{
	print("\n$num is even.\n");
}
```

<u>Output:</u>

```
Command Prompt
F:\PerlScripts>perl unlessdemo.pl
Enter an integer: 91
91 is odd.
F:\PerlScripts>perl unlessdemo.pl
Enter an integer: 28
28 is even.
F:\PerlScripts>
```

We have seen that using ***if-elsif-else***, we can check for multiple conditions. A similar thing can be done using ***unless-elsif-else*** blocks. There will be a mandatory ***unless block***, then there could be multiple ***elsifblocks*** followed by an optional ***else block***. This is how such a combination will work – the condition of the ***unless statement*** will be evaluated. If it evaluates to ***false***, the ***unless block*** will be executed, rest of the blocks will be skipped. If it evaluates to ***true***, the ***unless block*** will be skipped and the execution control will jump to the first ***elsif*** block, its condition will be checked and if it evaluates to ***true***, that particular ***elsif block*** will be executed. This process will go on until an ***elsif block*** with a valid condition is found or there are no more ***elsif blocks*** left. If there is no ***elsif block*** with a condition that evaluates to ***true***, the ***else block*** (if present) will be executed. Refer to the following snippet in order to understand this concept in a better way:

```
unless ( <condition 1>)
{
        #This block will be executed if <condition 1> is NOT true.
        #Statements…
}
elsif ( <condition 2> )
{
        #This block will be executed if <condition 1> is true
        <condition 2> is true.
        #Statements…
}
elsif ( <condition 3> )
{
        #This block will be executed if <condition 1> is true
        <condition 2> is false and <condition 3> is true.
        #Statements…
}
else
{
        #This block will be executed if <condition 1> is true and
<condition 2> and                    <condition 3> are false.
        #Statements…
}
```

Let us re-write the program to determine whether a number is positive, negative or zero using ***unless-elsif-else*** combination:

```
#Unless-ElsIf-Else demo. Check if a number is positive,
negative or zero
print ("\nEnter a number: ");
#Use prompt to receive the input into variable $num
#Use chomp at the time of taking input.
chomp ($num = <STDIN>);
#Check if the number is NOT greater than or equal to 0.
#If so, it is negative
unless ($num >= 0)
{
	print("\n$num is negative.\n");
}
#Check if the number is greater than 0.
#If so, it is positive
elsif ($num > 0)
{
	print("\n$num is positive.\n");
}
#If the number is neither positive nor negative, means
it is zero.
else
{
	print ("\n$num is zero.\n")
}
```

Output:

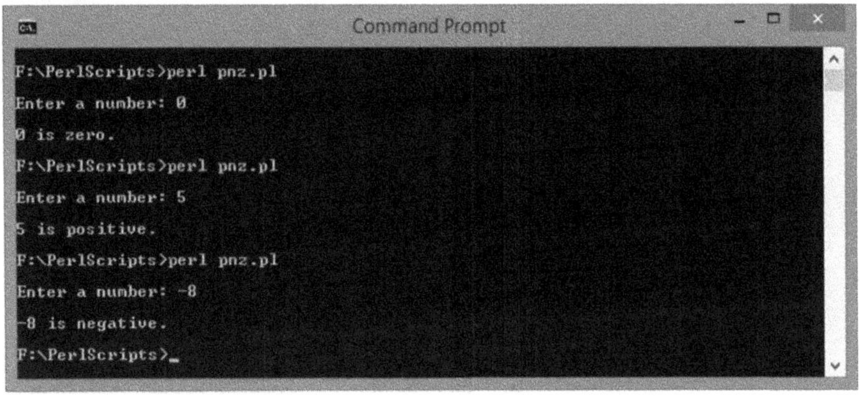

```
Command Prompt

F:\PerlScripts>perl pnz.pl
Enter a number: 0
0 is zero.
F:\PerlScripts>perl pnz.pl
Enter a number: 5
5 is positive.
F:\PerlScripts>perl pnz.pl
Enter a number: -8
-8 is negative.
F:\PerlScripts>_
```

Notes:

1. An ***unless-block*** can be standalone and the ***unless-statement*** should be supplied with a condition.
2. Other than ***elsif*** blocks, there should be no other statements sandwiched between an ***unless block*** and an ***else block***.
3. When an ***unless block*** is followed by multiple ***elsif*** blocks, ***ONLY ONE*** of all of these blocks will be executed depending on whether one or more conditions are true or not true. When a particular block is done executing, rest of the blocks will be skipped.

10. Loops

Loops are ***Control Structures*** which are used to run a piece of code over and over again as long as a particular condition is met (or not met). Perl offers the following loops – ***while***, ***do while***, ***for***, ***foreach*** and ***until***. Out of these, the ***foreach*** loop will be covered in the next chapter.

10.1 while Loop

The ***while loop*** keeps executing the statements present inside the ***while block*** over and over as long as the given condition evaluates to ***true***. General syntax:

```
while (<condition>)
{
        #Statements to be executed as long as <condition> is true.
}
```

Example:

```
$count = 0;
while ($count < 5)
{
        print ("Count: $count\n");
        $count++;
}
```

When a ***while statement*** is encountered, its ***condition*** is checked. If it evaluates to ***true***, the statements inside the ***while block*** are executed on by one. This is known as one loop ***iteration***. When the end of the block is reached, the execution control will jump back to the ***while statement*** and check the condition again, if it evaluates to ***true*** again, the block will be executed one more time. This process will go on as long as the condition evaluates to ***true***. The moment the given condition evaluates to ***false***, the execution control will come out of the ***while block***. If the condition never evaluates to ***false***, the loop will go on executing indefinitely and such as loop is also known as an ***infinite loop***. In order to keep track of the execution of the loop, we can use a ***loop variable***. This is not mandatory, but it makes logical sense. In the above code snippet, we initialize a variable called ***$count to 0***. We run the loop for as long as ***$count is less than 5***. This means, the loop will stop executing when ***$count becomes 5***. This variable ***$count*** is our loop variable as it will be used to keep track of the numbers of iterations this loop will go through.

Note: If you are ever stuck in an infinite loop, press CTRL + C to come out of it.

Let us write a program to display numbers from 1 to 10 using while loop:

```
#while loop demo
#Initialize a variable to 1
$number = 1;
#Loop from 1 to 10
while ($number <= 10)
{
	#Display number
	print ("\n$number");
	#Increment number
	$number++;
}
print ("\n");
```

Output:

```
Command Prompt
F:\PerlScripts>perl whiledemo.pl
1
2
3
4
5
6
7
8
9
10
F:\PerlScripts>
```

10.2 do-while Loop

The ***do-while loop*** is similar to the ***while loop*** and will keep on executing the loop block as long as the given ***condition*** is ***true***. General Syntax:

```
do
{
        #Statements to be executed as long as <condition> is true.
} while (<condition>);
```

Example:

```
$count = 0;
do
{
        print (“Count: $count\n”);
        $count++;
} while ($count < 5);
```

The difference between ***while*** and ***do-while*** loops is that instead of checking the condition at the beginning, the ***do-while loop*** checks the condition at the end of the loop block (as seen from the general syntax). As a result, the ***do-while*** loop is guaranteed to execute at least once even if the condition is ***false***. Let us write a Perl script to display numbers from 10 to 1 in a descending order:

```
#do-while loop demo
#Initialize a variable to 10
$number = 10;
#Loop from 10 to 1, check the condition at the end.
do
{
      #Display number
      print ("\n$number");
      #Decrement number
      $number--;
} while($number >= 1);

print ("\n");
```

Output:

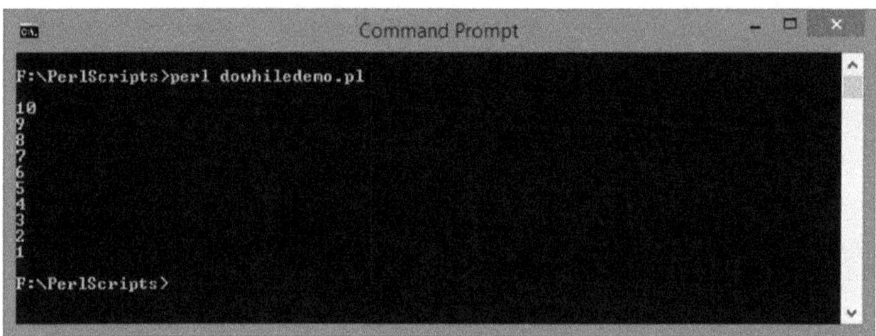

10.3 until Loop

Unlike ***while*** and ***do-while*** loops, the ***until loop*** keeps on executing the loop block as long as the given ***condition*** is ***NOT true***. General Syntax:

until (<condition>)

{

#Statements to be executed as long as <condition> is false.

}

Example:

$n = -5;

until ($n == 0)

{

print (“\nn = $n”);

$n++;

}

Let us write a Perl script to print multiples of 5, from 5 to 50:

```
#until loop demo
#Initialize a variable to 1
$number = 1;
#Loop until number becomes 11
#This loop will run till number becomes 10
until ($number == 11)
{
	#Display number
	print ($number * 5);
	print ("\n");
	#Increment number
	$number++;
}
```

Output:

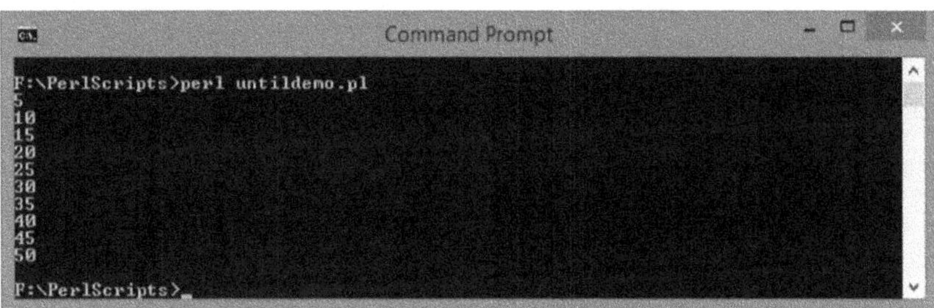

10.4 for Loop

The ***for loop*** keeps iterating as long as the given condition evaluates to ***true*** but has more features. It allows you to initialize the loop variable, check for the condition and increment/decrement the loop variable all in one statement. Here is the general syntax:

for (<variable initialization>;<condition>;<increment/ decrement>)

{

#Statements to be executed as long as the <condition> is true.

}

for ($i = 0 ; i < 10 ; i ++)

{

print ("\n$i");

}

Let us write a program using ***for loop*** to find the values of this polynomial –> $x^2 + 3x + 2$ for *x = -5 to x = 5.*

```
#for loop demo
#Run for loop from x = -5 to x = 5
for ($x = -5 ; $x <= 5 ; $x++)
{
	#Calculate the value of the polynomial for x
	$value = ($x * $x) + (3 * x) + 2;
	#Print x and value
	print ("\nx = $x \t\tvalue = $value");
}
print ("\n");
```

Output:

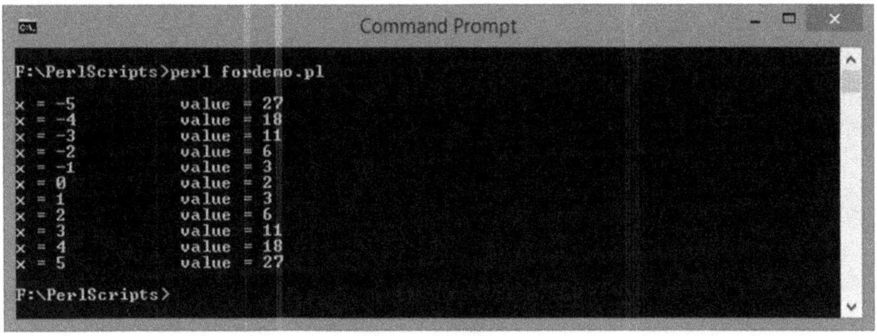

```
Command Prompt

F:\PerlScripts>perl fordemo.pl
x = -5          value = 27
x = -4          value = 18
x = -3          value = 11
x = -2          value = 6
x = -1          value = 3
x = 0           value = 2
x = 1           value = 3
x = 2           value = 6
x = 3           value = 11
x = 4           value = 18
x = 5           value = 27

F:\PerlScripts>
```

Let us take another programming example where we will ask the user to enter a number and calculate its factorial. ***Factorial*** of a number ***n*** is given by ***n!*** where $n! = n \times (n - 1) \times (n - 2) \times \ldots 1$. This can also be written in a recursive manner as $n! = n \times (n - 1)!$. Factorial of a negative number cannot be calculated and ***factorial of 0 is 1***. Let us take an example. ***Factorial of 4*** is given by $4! = 4 \times 3 \times 2 \times 1 = 24$. Here is the Perl script:

```
#Factorial demo.
print ("\nEnter a number: ");
#Use prompt to receive the input into variable $num
#Use chomp at the time of taking input.
chomp ($num = <STDIN>);
#Initialize factorial to 1
$fact = 1;
#Run loop from num to 1
for ($i = $num ; $i > 0 ; $i--)
{
      $fact = $fact * $i;
}
#Display result
print("\nFactorial: $fact\n");
```

Output:

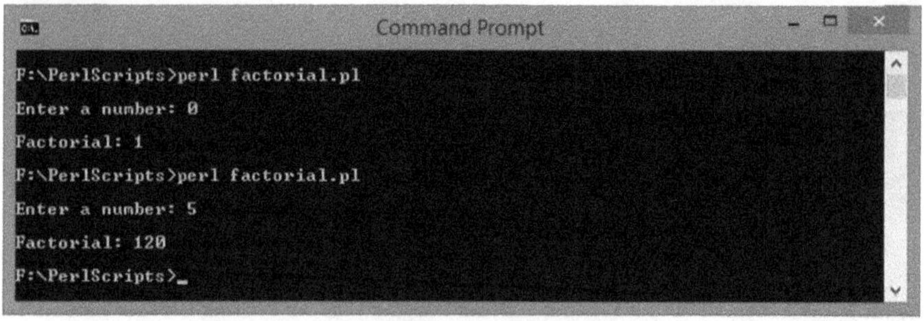

```
Command Prompt
F:\PerlScripts>perl factorial.pl
Enter a number: 0
Factorial: 1
F:\PerlScripts>perl factorial.pl
Enter a number: 5
Factorial: 120
F:\PerlScripts>_
```

10.5 Nested Loops

Loops can be placed inside one another. This process is known as nesting of loops. You can go for any level of nesting. Let us programmatically print the following number pattern using nested loops:

1

2 1

3 2 1

4 3 2 1

5 4 3 2 1

6 5 4 3 2 1

7 6 5 4 3 2 1

We will use two for loops, the outer loop will take care of the rows and the inner one will take care of the columns:

```
#Nesting Demo
#Outer Loop
for ($i = 1 ; $i <= 7 ; $i++)
{
	#Inner Loop
	for ($j = $i ; $j >= 1 ; $j--)
```

```
        {
                print ("$j ");
        }
        print("\n");
}
```

Output:

```
Command Prompt
F:\PerlScripts>perl patterngen.pl
1
2 1
3 2 1
4 3 2 1
5 4 3 2 1
6 5 4 3 2 1
7 6 5 4 3 2 1

F:\PerlScripts>
```

10.6 Control Statements

Depending on the type of the loop, as long as the given condition is met or not met, the loop will go on iterating. Control statements are used to alter this linear execution pattern of loops. Let us take a look at the control statements that Perl offers.

10.6.1 next Statement

The ***next statement*** is used to force the loop into beginning the next iteration. When ***next statement*** is encountered, the remaining statements after this statement will be skipped and the execution control will jump to the beginning of the loop where the condition will be checked and the next iteration will begin. In case of ***for loop***, the loop variable will be incremented/decremented and then the condition will be checked. In case of other loops, only the condition will be checked and the next iteration will begin. Taking care of the loop variable's increment/decrement will have to be done separately otherwise the script may end up being unstable.

Let us understand how the ***next statement*** works with an example. Let us display numbers from 1 to 20 and skip numbers which are multiples of 3. Here is how to do it:

```
#Control Statements Demo - next
#Run for loop from 1 to 20
for ($num = 1 ; $num <= 20 ; $num++)
{
        #Check if num is a multiple of 3
        if ($num %3 == 0)
        {
                #Skip this iteration, go to next one
                next;
        }
        #Print num
        print ("\n$num");
}
print ("\n");
```

Output:

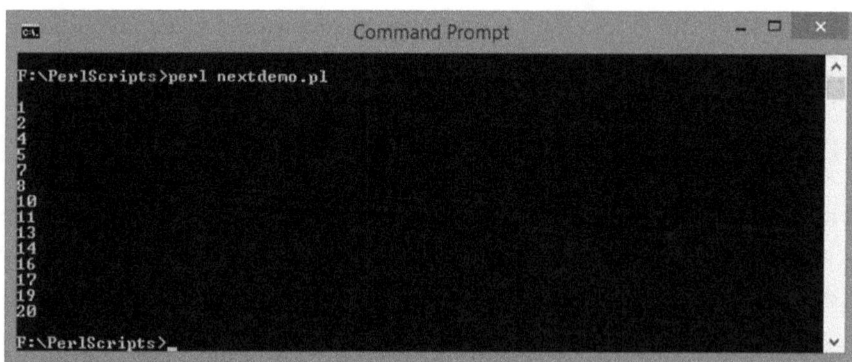

10.6.2 last Statement

The ***last statement*** is used to terminate the loop. When this statement is encountered, the execution control will come out of the loop. Here is a Perl script that demonstrated the usage of ***last statement***. There is a loop which counts from 0 to 9 but when the count reaches 5, we break out of the loop using ***last statement***.

```
#Control Statements Demo - last
#Run for loop from 0 to 9
$count = 0;

while ($count < 9)
{
      #Check if count is 5
      if ($count == 5)
      {
            #Come out of the loop
            last;
      }
      #Print count
      print ("\n$count");
      #Increment count
      $count++;
}
print ("\n");
```

Output:

```
F:\PerlScripts>perl lastdemo.pl

0
1
2
3
4

F:\PerlScripts>_
```

10.6.3 continue block

The ***continue block*** is placed soon after the end of the loop block and gets executed just before the condition is checked before the next iteration. This block is an ideal place to take care of the loop variable. The continue block can work with ***while loop***, ***until loop*** and ***foreach loop***. Here is the general syntax:

```
#While
while (<condition>)
{
```

#Statements

}

continue

{

#Statements

#Increment/Decrement loop variable

}

#Until

until (<condition>)

{

#Statements

}

continue

{

#Statements

#Increment/Decrement loop variable

}

Here is a script where we print numbers from 5 to 1 in a descending order. We decrement the loop variable inside the continue block:

```
#Loop Control - continue
$i = 5;
#Loop as long as i is not 0
until ($i == 0)
{
	#Print i
	print ("\n$i\n");
}
```

```
continue
{
	#Decrement i inside the continue block
	$i--;
}
```

Output:

```
F:\PerlScripts>perl continuedemo.pl
5
4
3
2
1
F:\PerlScripts>_
```

10.6.4 redo Statement

If there is ever a need to restart the current iteration of the loop, ***redo statement*** can be used. When a ***redo statement*** is encountered, the execution control will jump to the beginning of the loop without checking the condition again. Let us take an example where we will count from 0 to 9 using a ***for loop*** and reset the loop when count reaches 7.

```
#Control Statements Demo - redo
#Run for loop from 0 to 9
for ($num = 0 ; $num < 10 ; $num++)
{
	#Print num
	print ("\n$num");
	if ($num == 7)
	{
		redo;
	}

}
print ("\n");
```

When ***$num*** is going from ***0 to 6***, it will be printed normally. When ***$num reaches 7***, it will be printed and the ***if block*** will get executed (because ***$num == 7*** will evaluate to ***true***) that will force the loop to start the current iteration again. Without checking the condition and without incrementing ***$num***, the iteration will restart where it will print ***$num***, check ***if $num is 7*** (which will be ***true*** forever from hereon because we there is no other statement that increments ***$num***) and restart the iteration. This process will go on indefinitely and this loop will qualify as an ***infinite loop***. Here is what you will see:

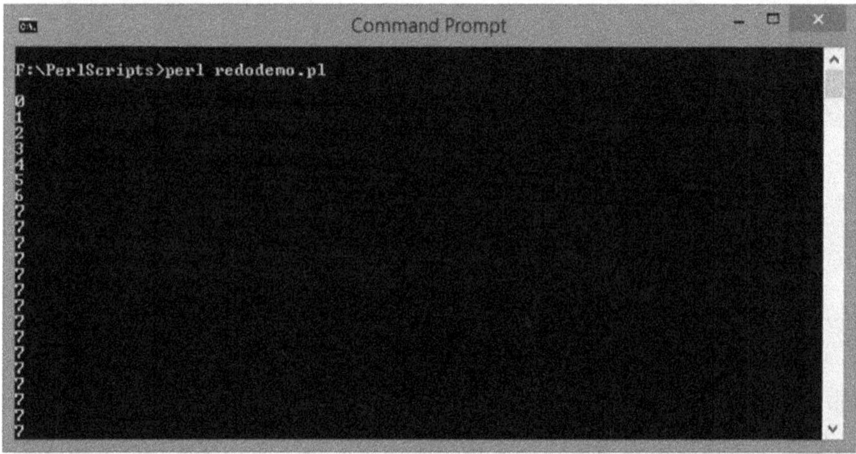

Pressing ***CTRL + C*** will get you out of this infinite loop:

Now, if you want to get something meaningful out of the ***redo statement***, you have to ***increment/decrement*** the loop variable separately. Let us modify the above code to count from 0 to 9 and skip printing 5 using the ***redo statement***:

```
#Control Statements Demo - redo
#Run for loop from 0 to 9
for ($num = 0 ; $num < 10 ; $num++)
{
      if ($num == 5)
      {
            $num++;
            redo;
      }
      #Print num
      print ("\n$num");
}
print ("\n");
```

Output:

In case a ***continue block*** is used alongside a ***while/until loop***, the ***redo statement*** will skip the ***continue block*** where the loop variable is usually incremented or decremented. Here is an example where we count from 0 to 9 and reset the iteration at 6:

```
#Control Statements Demo - redo/continue
#Run for loop from 0 to 9
$num = 0;
while ($num < 10)
{

      #Reset at 6
```

```
        if ($num == 6)
        {
                redo;
        }
        #Print num
        print ("\nInside while block - $num");
}
continue
{
        $num = $num + 1;
        print ("\nInside continue block - $num");
}
print ("\n");
```

<u>Output:</u>

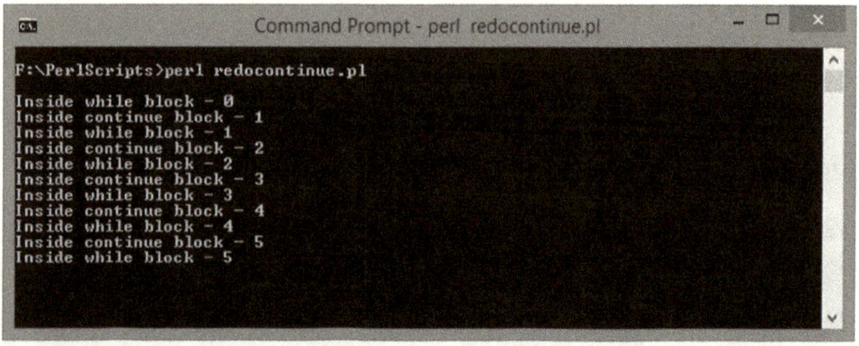

```
Command Prompt - perl redocontinue.pl

F:\PerlScripts>perl redocontinue.pl

Inside while block - 0
Inside continue block - 1
Inside while block - 1
Inside continue block - 2
Inside while block - 2
Inside continue block - 3
Inside while block - 3
Inside continue block - 4
Inside while block - 4
Inside continue block - 5
Inside while block - 5
```

As seen, the script gets stuck when 5 is printed because when ***$num*** becomes 6, the iteration is restarted there by skipping the continue block which used to increment ***$num***. Incrementing ***$num*** inside the ***if-block*** will solve this problem. In this case, the loop will skip printing 6 inside the loop block but will do so in the ***continue block***:

```
#Control Statements Demo - redo/continue
#Run for loop from 0 to 9
$num = 0;
while ($num < 10)
{

        #Reset at 6
        if ($num == 6)
        {
                $num++;
```

```
                redo;
        }
        #Print num
        print ("\nInside while block - $num");
}
continue
{
        $num = $num + 1;
        print ("\nInside continue block - $num");
}
print ("\n");
```

Output:

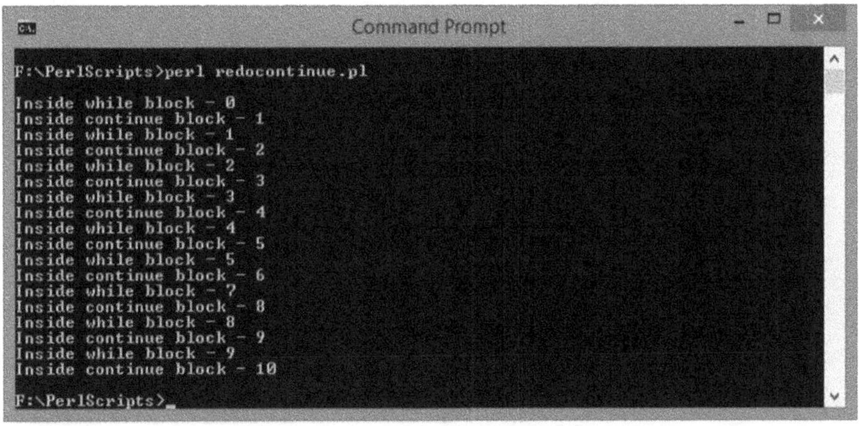

```
F:\PerlScripts>perl redocontinue.pl

Inside while block - 0
Inside continue block - 1
Inside while block - 1
Inside continue block - 2
Inside while block - 2
Inside continue block - 3
Inside while block - 3
Inside continue block - 4
Inside while block - 4
Inside continue block - 5
Inside while block - 5
Inside continue block - 6
Inside while block - 7
Inside continue block - 8
Inside while block - 8
Inside continue block - 9
Inside while block - 9
Inside continue block - 10

F:\PerlScripts>_
```

The ***foreach loop*** has been kept out of this chapter on purpose because, in order to understand the working of this loop, some knowledge of ***Arrays*** is required. Loops in general are very useful in many situations especially when working with arrays. Hence it is recommended that you understand this chapter thoroughly before proceeding to the next one.

11. Arrays

An array is a collection of elements. An element can be of any scalar type such as numbers or strings. A collection of mixed data types is permitted but it is best to stick to a collection of a single data type unless you absolutely have to mix different data types. Elements of an array can be uniquely addressed using ***index*** which begins at ***0*** and ends at ***1 less than the size of the array***. For example, if there is an array of 10 elements, the first element will be present at index 0, the second one at index 1, the third one at index 2 and so on; the last element will be present at index 9.

11.1 Array Creation

Array variables begin with ***@ sign*** as opposed to ***$ sign*** in case of scalar variables. An array can be created by enclosing the list of elements within parenthesis where each element is separated by a comma. General Syntax:

@<array variable> = (<elements separated by comma>);

Example:

@numbers = (5, 0.7, 6.3, -2, 55);

@names = ("Isla", "Ester", "Fido");

@mix = (3, "Tom", -6.54, "UK");

In the above examples, the indices and corresponding elements are listed below:

@numbers array:

Index 0 – 5

Index 1 – 0.7

Index 2 – 6.3

Index 3 – -2

Index 4 – 55

Here is how ***@numbers*** array is going to look inside the memory:

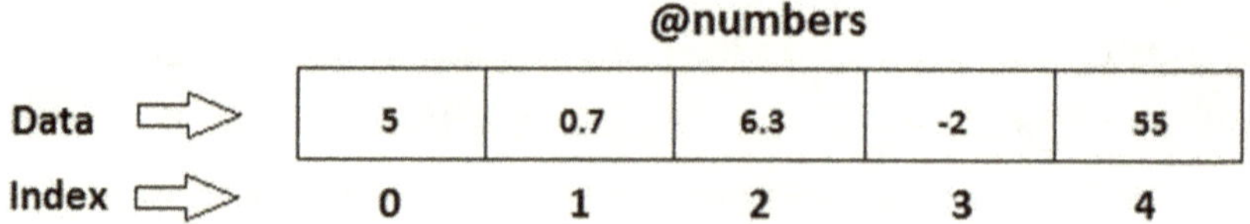

@names array:

Index 0 – "Isla"

Index 1 – "Ester"

Index 2 – "Fido"

Here is how ***@names*** array is going to look in the memory:

@names

	Isla	Ester	Fido
Data	Isla	Ester	Fido
Index	0	1	2

@mix array:

Index 0 – 3

Index 1 – "Tom"

Index 2 – -6.54

Index 3 – "UK"

Here is how ***@mix*** array is going to look in the memory:

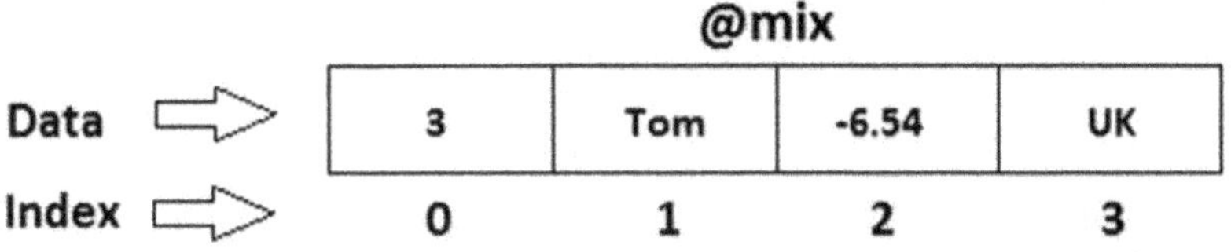

There is another way of creating an array using the ***qw*** function. General syntax:

@<array variable> = qw / <elements separated by space> /;

Example:

@x = qw /1 2 3 4 5/;

@msg = wq /Hello World/;

11.2 Accessing Array Elements

All the elements of an array can be accessed at once using the array variable. For example, if there is an array called ***@arr_1*** and you want to display all the elements of this array, you can simply use the print function like this – ***print (@arr_1);*** and all the elements will be printed.

Individual elements of an array can be accessed using the ***access operator ([ ])***. General Syntax:

$<array variable> [<index>]

Example:

$data = $x[1];

Consider the following array declaration:

@num = (8, 2, 9, -2, 6);

Element at 0 (value of 8) can be accessed as ***$num[0]***, ***element at 1*** (value of 2) can be accessed as ***$num[1]*** and so on. Since the size of this array is 5, the last element is at index 4. That is, ***$num[4]*** will refer to the value of *6*. Alternatively, the value at the last index can be accessed with the ***index -1*** (Eg. ***$num[-1]*** will refer to the last value of *6*). Note that while declaring an array, we use the ***@*** sign and while accessing individual elements, we use the ***$*** sign.

The maximum index of an array is given by:

$#<array variable>

Example:

$max_index = $#names;

The size of an array can be determined by the ***scalar*** keyword. General Syntax:

$<variable> = scalar @<array variable>;

Example:

$size = scalar @arr_1;

Let us write a Perl script that demonstrates the basic concepts of arrays – initializing arrays and accessing elements.

```
#Arrays Demo
#Declare a few arrays:
@num = (4, 7, -20.4, 5.764, -12, 8.84);
@country    =    ("Germany",    "Ethiopia",    "Poland",
"Singapore", "Brazil");
@temp = qw/16 23 19 32 11/;
@record = ("Dino", 29, "M", 68);
#Determine size and last index
$size_num = scalar @num;
$size_country = scalar @country;
$size_temp = scalar @temp;
$size_record = scalar @record;
$max_index_num = $#num;
$max_index_country = $#country;
$max_index_temp = $#temp;
$max_index_record = $#record;
#Display array contents together
```

```
print ("\n\@num: @num\nSize: $size_num Max Index: $max_index_num");
print ("\n\n\@country: @country\nSize: $size_country Max Index: $max_index_country");
print ("\n\n\@temp: @temp\nSize: $size_temp Max Index: $max_index_temp");
print ("\n\n\@record: @record\nSize: $size_record Max Index: $max_index_record\n");
#Display individual values of @num
print ("\n\@num values accessed individually:\n");
print ("\nValue at index 0: $num[0]");
print ("\nValue at index 1: $num[1]");
print ("\nValue at index 2: $num[2]");
print ("\nValue at index 3: $num[3]");
print ("\nValue at index 4: $num[4]");
print ("\nValue at index 5: $num[5]\n");
#Change values of @record
$record[0] = "Diorah";
$record[1] = 26;
$record[2] = "F";
$record[3] = 52;
#Display entire record array
print ("\n\@record array after updating its individual elements:\n\n@record\n");
```

Output:

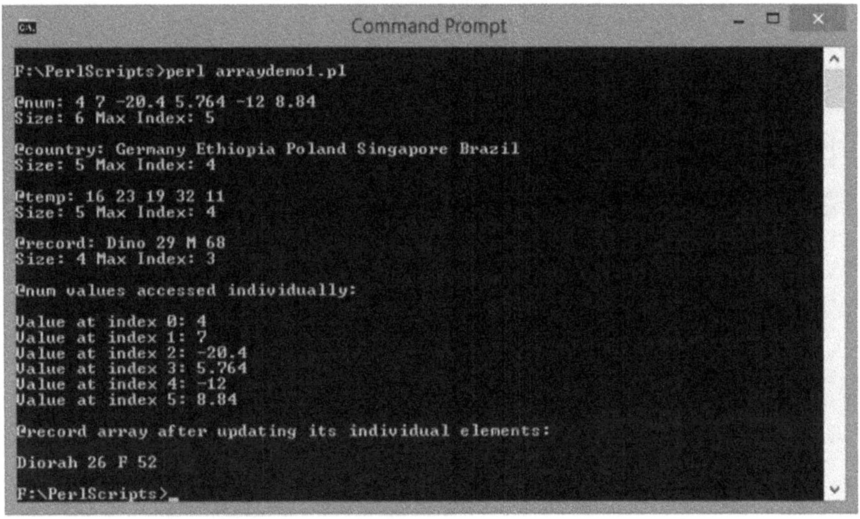

```
Command Prompt

F:\PerlScripts>perl arraydemo1.pl

@num: 4 7 -20.4 5.764 -12 8.84
Size: 6 Max Index: 5

@country: Germany Ethiopia Poland Singapore Brazil
Size: 5 Max Index: 4

@temp: 16 23 19 32 11
Size: 5 Max Index: 4

@record: Dino 29 M 68
Size: 4 Max Index: 3

@num values accessed individually:

Value at index 0: 4
Value at index 1: 7
Value at index 2: -20.4
Value at index 3: 5.764
Value at index 4: -12
Value at index 5: 8.84

@record array after updating its individual elements:

Diorah 26 F 52

F:\PerlScripts>_
```

11.3 Range Operator

The range operator is given by ***double dots (..)*** and can be used to fill arrays sequentially with numbers or letters. General Syntax:

@<array variable> = (<starting sequence> … <ending sequence>);

Example:

@x = (0 .. 5);

@m = (A .. Z);

Here is a script that demonstrates the usage of this operator:

```
#Range Operator Demo
#Fill array with numbers from 1 to 20
@num_array_1 = (1 .. 20);
#Fill array with alphabets from A to Z
@alpha_array_1 = (A .. Z);
#Fill array with numbers from -5 to +5
@num_array_2 = (-5 .. 5);
#Fill array with alphabets from p to z
@alpha_array_2 = (p .. z);
#Display everything
print ("\nnum_array_1:\n@num_array_1\n");
print ("\nnum_array_2:\n@num_array_2\n");
print ("\nalpha_array_1:\n@alpha_array_1\n");
print ("\nalpha_array_2:\n@alpha_array_2\n");
```

Output:

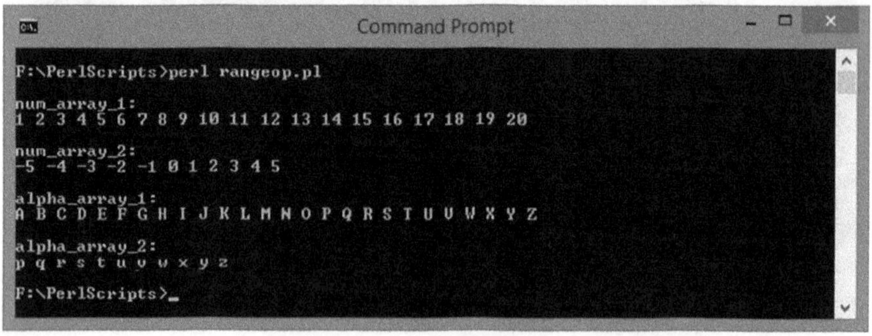

```
Command Prompt
F:\PerlScripts>perl rangeop.pl

num_array_1:
1 2 3 4 5 6 7 8 9 10 11 12 13 14 15 16 17 18 19 20

num_array_2:
-5 -4 -3 -2 -1 0 1 2 3 4 5

alpha_array_1:
A B C D E F G H I J K L M N O P Q R S T U V W X Y Z

alpha_array_2:
p q r s t u v w x y z

F:\PerlScripts>_
```

Note: The range operator will fill an array in ascending order only. Hence, the start sequence should be less than the end sequence in case of numbers and in case of alphabets, the start sequence should appear earlier than the end sequence with respect to the alphabetical order.

11.4 Arrays and Loops

Loops are very useful when it comes to working with arrays. We know that the index of an array begins at 0 and goes up to ***size - 1***. This makes an ideal case for accessing arrays with loops. If we initialize a loop variable to 0 and set the condition of the loop as the loop variable should increment up to ***size - 1***, we can iterate through the whole array one index at a time. Here is a script where we initialize a few arrays and display their contents using loops:

```
#Array Access with Loops
#Initialize a few arrays:
#Fill array with numbers from 10 to 15
@num_array = (10 .. 15);
#Create an array of strings
@food_items = ("Pasta", "Tortilla", "Ful", "Pad Thai");
#Array of random numbers
@x = (6.8, -4.56, 0, 31, 22, -23.4, 9);
#Determine size of each array
$size_num_array = scalar @num_array;
$size_food_items = scalar @food_items;
$size_x = scalar @x;
#Display elements of num_array using while loop
print ("\nDisplaying \@num_array using while loop: \n");
$i = 0;
#Run the loop from 0 to size_num_array - 1
while ($i < $size_num_array)
{
      print     ("\nIndex:     $i\t\@num_array[$i]      =
$num_array[$i]");
      #Increment $i
      $i = $i + 1;
}
```

```
print ("\n\nDisplaying \@food_items using until loop: \n");
$i = 0;
#Run the loop from 0 to size_food_items - 1
until ($i == $size_food_items)
{
	print ("\nIndex: $i\t\@food_items[$i] = $food_items[$i]");
	#Increment $i
	$i++;
}
print ("\n\nDisplaying \@x using loop: \n");
#Run the loop from 0 to size_x - 1
for ($j = 0 ; $j < $size_x ; $j++)
{
	print ("\nIndex: $j\t\@x[$j] = $x[$j]");
}
print ("\n");
```

<u>Output:</u>

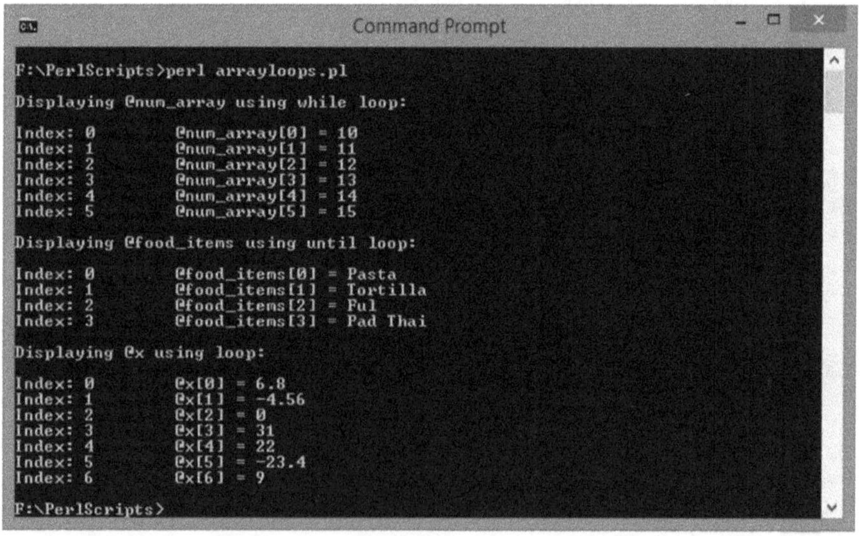

```
Command Prompt

F:\PerlScripts>perl arrayloops.pl

Displaying @num_array using while loop:

Index: 0        @num_array[0] = 10
Index: 1        @num_array[1] = 11
Index: 2        @num_array[2] = 12
Index: 3        @num_array[3] = 13
Index: 4        @num_array[4] = 14
Index: 5        @num_array[5] = 15

Displaying @food_items using until loop:

Index: 0        @food_items[0] = Pasta
Index: 1        @food_items[1] = Tortilla
Index: 2        @food_items[2] = Ful
Index: 3        @food_items[3] = Pad Thai

Displaying @x using loop:

Index: 0        @x[0] = 6.8
Index: 1        @x[1] = -4.56
Index: 2        @x[2] = 0
Index: 3        @x[3] = 31
Index: 4        @x[4] = 22
Index: 5        @x[5] = -23.4
Index: 6        @x[6] = 9

F:\PerlScripts>
```

11.5 foreach Loop

In the previous chapter, ***foreach*** loop was excluded on purpose because it works only on lists such as arrays. General syntax of this loop is:

foreach $<element> (@<array_variable>)

{

#Statements...

}

Example:

@x = (6, 2, 9);

foreach $num (@x)

{

print ($num);

}

An element from the array will be fetched and assigned to ***$<element>*** scalar variable during each iteration of the loop starting from the first element of the array (at index 0). During the next iteration, the next element will be fetched. This process will go on happening until the last element is fetched. Instead of accessing the array elements using their index, the ***foreach*** loop offers a simpler way. The number of times a ***foreach*** loop will iterate will be equal to the number of elements present in the array. Here is a sample script:

```
#Foreach loop demo
#Initialize an array
@arr = (8, -2.6, 7.12, 8.32, -3, 5);
#Variable to count the number of iterations
$count = 0;
#Loop through the array
foreach $element (@arr)
{
	print ("\nIteration: $count\tItem: $element");
	$count++;
}
print ("\n");
```

Output:

```
Command Prompt

F:\PerlScripts>perl foreachdemo.pl

Iteration: 0     Item: 8
Iteration: 1     Item: -2.6
Iteration: 2     Item: 7.12
Iteration: 3     Item: 8.32
Iteration: 4     Item: -3
Iteration: 5     Item: 5

F:\PerlScripts>
```

11.6 Reading user input into arrays

If you want to read multiple inputs from the user and store in an array, you can use prompt inside a loop. This will give an opportunity to the user to give inputs as many times as the loop runs. Here is a script that does exactly this:

```
#Reading user input into an array
#Create a blank array
@arr = ();
#Run for loop 5 times
for ($i = 0 ; $i < 5 ; $i++)
{
      print ("\nEnter element at index $i: ");
      #Read input, chomp it
      chomp ($num = (<>));
      #Store it in the array
      $arr[$i] = $num;
}
#Display the array
for ($i = 0 ; $i < 5 ; $i++)
{
      print ("\nIndex: $i\t\@arr[$i] = $arr[$i]");
}
print ("\n");
```

Output:

```
Command Prompt

F:\PerlScripts>perl arrayinput.pl
Enter element at index 0: 8
Enter element at index 1: 1
Enter element at index 2: 6
Enter element at index 3: 7
Enter element at index 4: 3
Index: 0        @arr[0] = 8
Index: 1        @arr[1] = 1
Index: 2        @arr[2] = 6
Index: 3        @arr[3] = 7
Index: 4        @arr[4] = 3

F:\PerlScripts>
```

11.7 Array Manipulation

We have seen that individual elements of an array can be accessed with its index. With this, we can retrieve the element as well as update it. Let us recap how we can do this:

Retrieve a value:

$<variable> = $<array variable>[<index];

Example:

$x = $arr[4];

Set an element:

$<array variable>[<index] = <value>;

Example:

$arr[2] = 50.67;

The last index of the array is 1 less than its size. Say there is an array of 3 elements. Consider the following declaration:

@x = (2, 7, 4);

The array ***x*** has 3 elements, the first index is 0 and the last index is 2. Say, you try to set an index which is greater than its last index such as index 7. This will still be valid. The size of the array will become 7 and the value you tried to set will be present at index 6 and from index 3 to index 5, the array will have NULL value. Here is a script that shows this:

```
#Array index out of bounds
#Declare an array of 5 elements
@arr = (5, 8, 1, -2, 3);
#Print array size
print("\nArray size: ", scalar @arr, "\n");
#Display the array
for ($i = 0 ; $i < scalar @arr ; $i++)
{
      print ("\nIndex: $i\t\@arr[$i] = $arr[$i]");
}
#Add new value at index 9
$arr[9] = 7;
#Print array size
print("\n\nNew size: ", scalar @arr , "\n");
#Display the array
for ($i = 0 ; $i < scalar @arr ; $i++)
{
      print ("\nIndex: $i\t\@arr[$i] = $arr[$i]");
}
print ("\n");
```

Output:

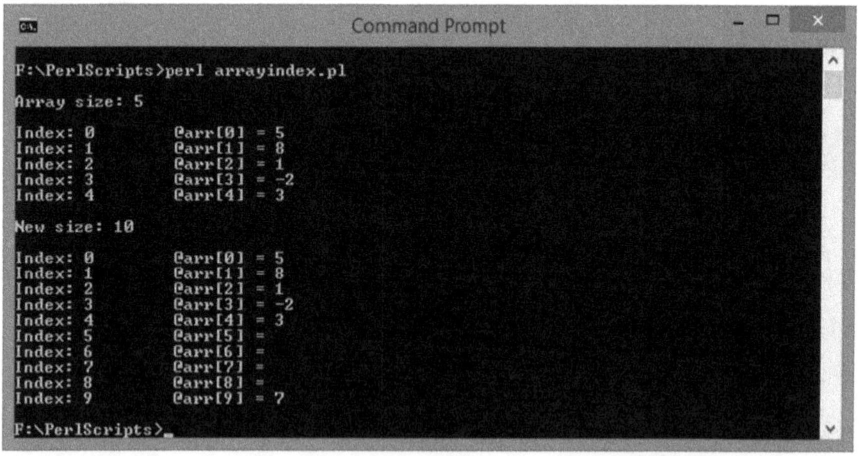

```
Command Prompt

F:\PerlScripts>perl arrayindex.pl

Array size: 5

Index: 0        @arr[0] = 5
Index: 1        @arr[1] = 8
Index: 2        @arr[2] = 1
Index: 3        @arr[3] = -2
Index: 4        @arr[4] = 3

New size: 10

Index: 0        @arr[0] = 5
Index: 1        @arr[1] = 8
Index: 2        @arr[2] = 1
Index: 3        @arr[3] = -2
Index: 4        @arr[4] = 3
Index: 5        @arr[5] =
Index: 6        @arr[6] =
Index: 7        @arr[7] =
Index: 8        @arr[8] =
Index: 9        @arr[9] = 7

F:\PerlScripts>_
```

As seen, when the array is first declared with 5 elements, index runs from 0 to 5. A new element is inserted at index 9, size now becomes 10 and there is NULL data at index 5 to index 8.

This is not a good way to add new elements to an existing array although it works and may be well suited in certain rare situations. A better way to add new elements to an array is to use the ***push*** function. General Syntax:

push (@<existing array variable>, <new element/list/another array>);

Example:

push (@arr, 6);

The ***push*** function will append the specified element/list to the existing array thereby increasing its size by 1 in case only one element is added and in case a list is added, the new size will be ***previous size + size of the new list.***

If you want to remove the last element, you can use the ***pop*** function. General Syntax:

pop (@<existing array variable>);

Example:

pop (@xyz);

The ***pop*** function will delete the element present at the last index and reduce the size of the array by 1.

Let us write a Perl script to demonstrate the usage of push and pop functions:

```
#Push Pop Demo
#Declare an array
@laptop = ("Lenovo", "HP", "Dell", "Asus");
```

```
#Print array size
print("\nArray size: ", scalar @laptop, "\n");
#Display the array
for ($i = 0 ; $i < scalar @laptop ; $i++)
{
	print ("\nIndex: $i\t\@laptop[$i] = $laptop[$i]");
}
#Push MSI to the array
push (@laptop, "MSI");
#Display the array again
#Print array size
print("\n\nAfter pushing MSI\nArray Size: ", scalar
@laptop, "\n");
#Display the array
for ($i = 0 ; $i < scalar @laptop ; $i++)
{
	print ("\nIndex: $i\t\@laptop[$i] = $laptop[$i]");
}
#POP 2 items
pop (@laptop);
pop (@laptop);
#Display the array again
#Print array size
print("\n\nAfter Popping 2 items\nArray Size: ", scalar
@laptop, "\n");
#Display the array
for ($i = 0 ; $i < scalar @laptop ; $i++)
{
	print ("\nIndex: $i\t\@laptop[$i] = $laptop[$i]");
}
#Create another array
@brands = ("Acer", "Gigabyte");
#Push @brands to @laptop
push (@laptop, @brands);
print("\n\nAfter pushing another array with values -
@brands\nArray Size: ", scalar @laptop, "\n");
#Display the array
for ($i = 0 ; $i < scalar @laptop ; $i++)
{
	print ("\nIndex: $i\t\@laptop[$i] = $laptop[$i]");
}
print ("\n");
```

Output:

```
Command Prompt
F:\PerlScripts>perl pushpop.pl
Array size: 4
Index: 0        @laptop[0] = Lenovo
Index: 1        @laptop[1] = HP
Index: 2        @laptop[2] = Dell
Index: 3        @laptop[3] = Asus
After pushing MSI
Array Size: 5
Index: 0        @laptop[0] = Lenovo
Index: 1        @laptop[1] = HP
Index: 2        @laptop[2] = Dell
Index: 3        @laptop[3] = Asus
Index: 4        @laptop[4] = MSI
After Popping 2 items
Array Size: 3
Index: 0        @laptop[0] = Lenovo
Index: 1        @laptop[1] = HP
Index: 2        @laptop[2] = Dell
After pushing another array with values - Acer Gigabyte
Array Size: 5
Index: 0        @laptop[0] = Lenovo
Index: 1        @laptop[1] = HP
Index: 2        @laptop[2] = Dell
Index: 3        @laptop[3] = Acer
Index: 4        @laptop[4] = Gigabyte
F:\PerlScripts>_
```

Merging two arrays can be done with ***push*** function as well as using the following syntax:

@<merged array> = (@<array 1>, @<array 2>, … @<array n>);

Example:

@x = (@a, @b, @c, @d);

11.8 Sorting Arrays

There is a function called ***sort*** which can be used to sort arrays with strings as well as numbers. General Syntax:

@<sorted array> = sort (@<array variable>);

Example:

@sorted_arr = sort (@arr);

This function will sort the array and return the new sorted array. There must be an array variable on the left hand side to receive the sorted array as shown above. In case an array has only numbers, the function will sort the numbers in ascending order. In case an array has a collection of strings, this function will sort according to the ***ASCII*** equivalent of the first character of each string. Strings starting with upper case letters will be sorted first and placed in the first half of the sorted array and strings starting with lower case first characters will be sorted and placed in the latter half of the sorted array. This is because, in the ***ASCII*** table, the upper case alphabet series starts at 65 (upper case 'A') and the lower case alphabet series (lower case 'a') starts at 97. In case there are numbers and strings with mixed cases, the numbers will be sorted and placed in the first part of the array, followed by sorted strings with upper case first characters and then the sorted strings with lower case first characters. Here is a Perl script that shows how the sort function works in different situations:

```
#Sorting Demo
#Declare a few arrays
@city = ("Tokyo", "Lexington", "Nairobi", "Auckland",
"Delhi");
@numbers = (5, 1, 9.6, -6.8, 12, 99, -4.23, 0, -8, 2);
@random_array = ("Singapore", 8, 2, -9.7, "zebra", 22,
"adam", -40, "Dillon", "Zanzibar", 989 );
#Print both arrays
print ("\n\@city array:\n\n@city");
print ("\n\n\@number array:\n\n@numbers");
print ("\n\n\@random_array:\n\n@@random_array");
#Sort both arrays using sort function
@new_city = sort (@city);
@new_numbers = sort (@numbers);
@new_random_array = sort (@random_array);
print ("\n\nArrays after sorting:\n");
print ("\n\@new_city array:\n\n@new_city");
print ("\n\n\@new_number array:\n\n@new_numbers");
print
("\n\n\@new_random_array:\n\n@new_random_array\n");
```

Output:

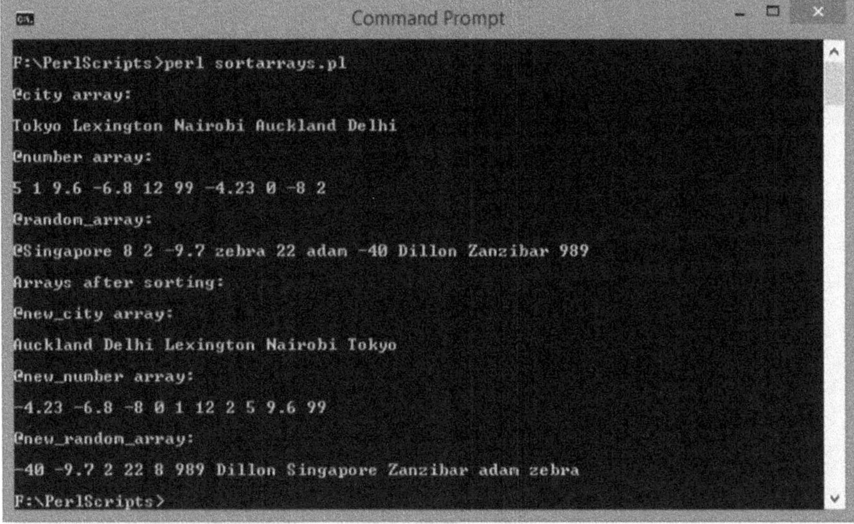
Command Prompt
F:\PerlScripts>perl sortarrays.pl
@city array:
Tokyo Lexington Nairobi Auckland Delhi
@number array:
5 1 9.6 -6.8 12 99 -4.23 0 -8 2
@random_array:
@Singapore 8 2 -9.7 zebra 22 adam -40 Dillon Zanzibar 989
Arrays after sorting:
@new_city array:
Auckland Delhi Lexington Nairobi Tokyo
@new_number array:
-4.23 -6.8 -8 0 1 12 2 5 9.6 99
@new_random_array:
-40 -9.7 2 22 8 989 Dillon Singapore Zanzibar adam zebra
F:\PerlScripts>

12. Hashes

Hashes are data structures which store data using ***key-value*** pairs. Hash variables begin with ***percentage sign (%)***. We can use the analogy of arrays to understand the concept of hashes. An array is a collection of elements where each element is present at an index that runs from 0 to size – 1. In case of a hash, a key can be looked at as a meaningful index and value could be looked at as an element at that meaningful index. Here is a general syntax of declaring hashes:

%<hash variable> = (<key 1>, <value 1>, <key 2>, <value 2>, … <key n>, value n>);

Example:

%person = (‘First Name’, ‘Rebecca’, ‘Last Name’, ‘Perry’, ‘Age’, 33, ‘Country’, ‘UK’);

There is a better syntax of creating hashes using **=>** character sequence for each key-value pair:

%<hash variable> = (<key 1> => <value 1>, … <key n> => value n>);

Example:

%employee = (‘emp_id’ => 12345, ‘emp_name’ => ‘Edward’, ‘emp_city’ => ‘NY’);

Let us take a look at the ***%person*** hash which stores personal information. Here are the keys and their corresponding values:

%person

key	value
‘First Name’	*‘Rebecca’*
‘Last Name’	*‘Perry’*
‘Age’	*33*
‘Country’	*‘UK’*

Here is how this hash will look inside memory:

%person

	'Rebecca'	'Perry'	33	'UK'
Value ⇨	'Rebecca'	'Perry'	33	'UK'
Key ⇨	'First Name'	'Last Name'	'Age'	'Country'

12.1 Accessing and Manipulating Hashes

Individual elements can be accessed using the following syntax:

$<variable> = $<hash variable>{<key>};

Example:

$name = $person{'First Name'};

Value for a particular key can be set using the following syntax:

$<hash variable>{<key>} = <value>;

Example:

$person{'Age'} = 34;

When we are setting a value for a particular key, if that key already exists, its value will be updated to the new one that we set and if that key does not exist, a new key-value pair will be created.

Note: While creating a hash variable, we use the ***percentage (%)*** sign for the variable name and while accessing key-value pairs, we use ***dollar ($)*** sign for the same variable name.

Let us write a Perl script and demonstrate whatever we have learnt in this chapter so far. We will create a hash called ***%person*** with personal information and display each ***key-value*** pair. We will then modify this hash by updating an existing ***key-value*** pair and also create a new pair.

```
#Hash Demo
#Create a hash
%person = ('First Name' => 'Rebecca', 'Last Name' =>'
Perry', 'Age' => 33, 'Country' => 'UK');
#Display all key-value pairs
print ("\n%person Hash\n\nFirst Name: $person{'First
Name'}");
print ("\nLast Name: $person{'Last Name'}");
print ("\nAge: $person{'Age'}");
print ("\nCountry: $person{'Country'}\n");
#Update Age
$person{'Age'} = 31;
#Add New key-value pair City - Manchester
$person{'City'} = "Manchester";
#Display Age and City
print ("\nAfter making changes to %person\n");
print ("\nAge: $person{'Age'}");
print ("\nCity: $person{'City'}\n");
```

Output:

```
F:\PerlScripts>perl hashdemo.pl

%person Hash

First Name: Rebecca
Last Name:  Perry
Age: 33
Country: UK

After making changes to %person

Age: 31
City: Manchester

F:\PerlScripts>_
```

Hashes can be created ***on-the-fly*** by dynamically assigning values to keys without previously declaring the hash variable. This is a very crude method and should be used only when you absolutely have to. Here is a small script which shows how hashes can be created ***on-the-fly***:

```
#Creating Hashes On-The-Fly
#Do not declare a hash element explicitly
#Create a key-value pair
$student{'student_id'} = 12345;
#Create another key-value pair
```

```
$student{'student_name'} = "Kyla";
#Create another hash variable on the fly
$home_appliance{'make'} = "LG";
#Create another key-value pair for the new hash
$home_applicance{'type'} = "4K LED TV";
#Display Everything
print ("\n%student Hash\n");
print ("\nstudent_id: $student{'student_id'}");
print ("\nstudent_name: $student{'student_name'}\n");
print ("\n\n%home_appliance Hash\n");
print ("\nmake: $home_appliance{'make'}");
print ("\ntype: $home_applicance{'type'} \n\n");
```

Output:

```
F:\PerlScripts>perl ontheflyhash.pl

%student Hash

student_id: 12345
student_name: Kyla


%home_appliance Hash

make: LG
type: 4K LED TV

F:\PerlScripts>_
```

12.1.1 Check if a Key Exists

Earlier on in this chapter, we saw that if you try to set value for an existing key, the old value will be replaced by new one and if you try to set value for a key that does not exist, a new key will be created. If you want to check if a key exists, you can use the ***exists*** function. This function will return ***true*** if the specified key exists and ***false*** if it does not. Here is the general syntax:

if (exists ($<hash variable>{<key>}))

{

#Statements to be executed if the specified key exists

}

Example:

if (exists ($car{'displacement'}))

{

print ("The key displacement exists for the hash %car");

}

12.1.2 Delete Hash Elements

A hash element can be deleted using the delete function. General syntax:

delete $<hash variable>{<key>};

Example:

delete $aircraft{'max_altitude'};

Let us write a Perl script to understand how ***exists*** and ***delete*** functions work:

```
#Hash - Check if key exists and Delete Demo
#Create a hash
%smartphone = ('make' => 'Google', 'model' => 'Pixel 4',
'chipset' => 'Snapdragon 855', 'sd_slot' => 'No');
#Display Everything
print ("\nHash - %smartphone\n");
print ("\nmake: $smartphone{'make'}");
print ("\nmodel: $smartphone{'model'}");
print ("\nchipset: $smartphone{'chipset'}");
print ("\nsd_slot: $smartphone{'sd_slot'}\n");
#Check if key chipset exists, if so, update it to
'Qualcomm Snapdragon 855'
if (exists ($smartphone{'chipset'}))
{
      print ("\nKey 'chipset' exists. Value -
$smartphone{'chipset'} . Updating new value... ...");
      $smartphone{'chipset'} = "Qualcomm Snapdragon
855";
      print ("\nNew value after updating 'chipset' key
- $smartphone{'chipset'}\n");
```

```
}
else
{
        print ("\nThe key 'chipset' does not exist.\n");
}
#Add some more key-value pairs
$smartphone{'ram'} = "8 GB";
$smartphone{'storage'} = "128 GB";
#Check if key sd_slot exists, if so, delete the key value
pair
if (exists ($smartphone{'sd_slot'}))
{
        print ("\nKey 'sd_slot' exists. Deleting the key-
value pair... ...");
        delete ($smartphone{'sd_slot'});
        print ("\nThe key 'sd_slot' has been deleted.\n");
}
else
{
        print ("\nThe key 'sd_slot' does not exist.\n");
}
#Display everything again
print ("\nHash - %smartphone\n");
print ("\nmake: $smartphone{'make'}");
print ("\nmodel: $smartphone{'model'}");
print ("\nchipset: $smartphone{'chipset'}");
print ("\nram: $smartphone{'ram'}");
print ("\nstorage: $smartphone{'storage'}\n");
```

<u>Output:</u>

```
Command Prompt

F:\PerlScripts>perl hashexistsdelete.pl

Hash - %smartphone

make: Google
model: Pixel 4
chipset: Snapdragon 855
sd_slot: No

Key 'chipset' exists. Value - Snapdragon 855 . Updating new value... ...
New value after updating 'chipset' key - Qualcomm Snapdragon 855

Key 'sd_slot' exists. Deleting the key-value pair... ...
The key 'sd_slot' has been deleted.

Hash - %smartphone

make: Google
model: Pixel 4
chipset: Qualcomm Snapdragon 855
ram: 8 GB
storage: 128 GB

F:\PerlScripts>
```

12.2 Fetch Keys and Values

Keys of a hash can be retrieved using the ***keys*** function. This function will return an array of keys of the specified hash. Here is the general syntax:

@<variable> = keys <hash variable>;

Example:

@person_keys = keys %person;

All the values of a hash can be fetched using the ***values*** function which will return an array of values of the specified hash. General syntax:

@<variable> = values <hash variable>;

Example:

@person_values = values %person;

Inside a hash, a key cannot exist without a value and a value cannot exist without a key. Hence it is safe to say that the number of keys will be equal to the number of values in a hash. Determining the array size of either keys or values should give us the size of the hash. Here is a script that demonstrates whatever we have learned in this section:

```
#Hash Keys Values
#Create a hash
%employee = ('employee_id' => 35675, 'First Name' =>
'Ashton', 'Last Name' =>'Root', 'Age' => 27, 'Country'
=> 'New Zealand');
#Display all key-value pairs
print ("\n%employee Hash\n\nemployee_id:
$employee{'employee_id'}");
print ("\nFirst Name: $employee{'First Name'}");
print ("\nLast Name: $employee{'Last Name'}");
print ("\nAge: $employee{'Age'}");
print ("\nCountry: $employee{'Country'}\n");
#Fetch all keys
```

```
@key_employee = keys %employee;
#Fetch all values
@value_employee = values %employee;
#Determine hash size by fetching size of key or value
array
$hash_size = scalar @key_employee;
#Display hash size, keys and values
print ("\n%employee hash size: $hash_size\n");
print ("\nKeys: \n@key_employee\n");
print ("\nValues: \n@value_employee\n");
```

Output:

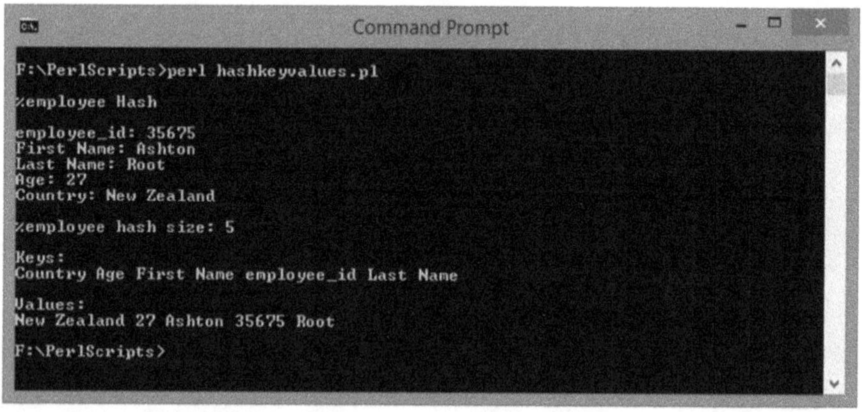

```
Command Prompt
F:\PerlScripts>perl hashkeyvalues.pl

%employee Hash

employee_id: 35675
First Name: Ashton
Last Name: Root
Age: 27
Country: New Zealand

%employee hash size: 5

Keys:
Country Age First Name employee_id Last Name

Values:
New Zealand 27 Ashton 35675 Root

F:\PerlScripts>
```

Hashes are very useful data structures that let you store data in key-value pairs. This opens up many possibilities. How you use hashes is left up to you. You can use them to store a record of one item where in many attributes such as name, address, age, etc. of a person can form a hash or you can use them to store one attribute of many items such as ages of different people.

13. Subroutines

A subroutine is a piece of reusable code. Subroutines are also known as functions, routines, methods or subs. So far, we have used built in subroutines such as ***print, chomp, sort,*** etc. These subroutines are defined by someone else, we were just using them. In this section, we will learn to write our own subroutines.

The topic of subroutines revolves around two major concepts – subroutine definition and subroutine call.

13.1 Defining a Subroutine

Subroutine definition is the core part. This is where the actual work gets done. This is the actual piece of reusable code that we talked about. A subroutine can be defined with using the ***sub*** keyword. General syntax:

```
sub <subroutine name>
{
        #Statements..
}
```

Example:

```
sub simpleSub
{
        print ("\nThis is just a demo sub!");
}
```

It is best to place all the user defined functions at the beginning of the script.

13.2 Calling a Subroutine

Merely defining a subroutine is not enough. It needs to be called so that the statements inside the definition start executing one by one. To call a subroutine, the following syntax is used:

<subroutine name> (<list of arguments separated by comma>);

Example:

myFunction( );

Data can be passed to a subroutine as arguments. We will learn more about passing values to a subroutine in the next section. Let us now write a simple subroutine and call it:

```
#Simple Subroutine Demo
#We'll have a subroutine that does not accept any parameters and does not return any value.
#Subroutine Definition
#Note that the script execution does not begin here
sub FirstSubroutine
{
	print ("\nWe are inside FirstSubroutine!\n");
}
#Execution of the script begins here
print ("\nScript execution has begun. Calling FirstSubroutine.\n");
#Call FirstSubroutine
FirstSubroutine();
print ("\nOutside FirstSubroutine. End of script.\n")
```

<u>Output:</u>

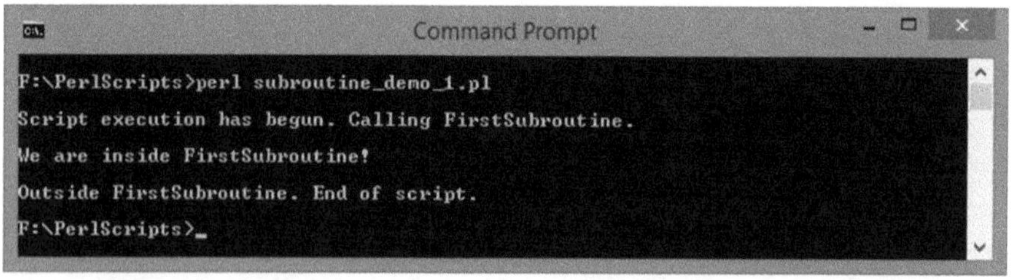

```
Command Prompt
F:\PerlScripts>perl subroutine_demo_1.pl
Script execution has begun. Calling FirstSubroutine.
We are inside FirstSubroutine!
Outside FirstSubroutine. End of script.
F:\PerlScripts>_
```

So far, we have learned that a Perl script starts executing from the first statement till the last one. In the above script, the first effective statement (leaving aside the comments) is ***sub FirstSubroutine*** but the Perl interpreter does not seem to be interested in executing what follows. This is because, subroutines can only execute once they are called and will not do so on their own. Refer to the following screenshot of the above code where the execution point has been marked:

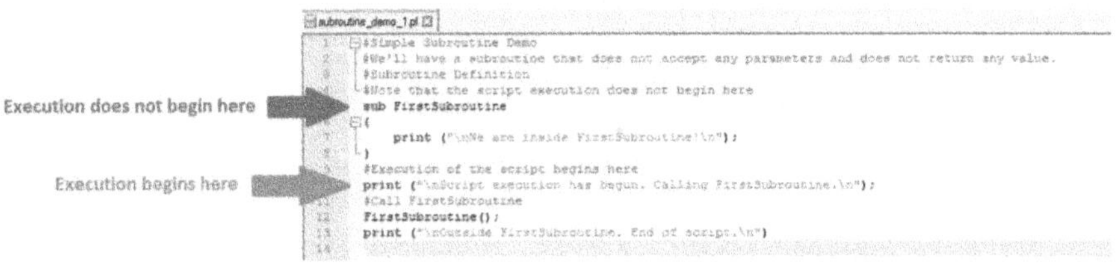

13.3 Passing arguments

Data can be passed to a function as arguments (also known as parameters). For example, when we use the ***print*** function, we pass a string as an argument. That string is received by the ***print*** function and then displayed. Arguments are passed to a subroutine during the time of subroutine call. You can pass as many arguments as you want separated by commas. Here is the general syntax:

<function name> (<argument 1>, <argument 2>, … <argument n>);

Example:

showData (6, "Norway", 7.9, -3.5, "Oslo", 0);

Now, here is the important part. When you pass arguments to a function, they are stored in a special array given by ***@_***. This array will store the arguments in the same order that they were passed. Individual elements of this array can be accessed as ***$_[<index>]***.

You can access the arguments using ***@_*** and ***$_[<index>]*** only from inside a function. Here is a simple script that demonstrates how to pass arguments and access them:

```
#Subroutine Demo - Passing Arguments
#We'll have a subroutine that accepts arguments but does not return any value
#Subroutine definition
sub ShowValues
{
	#Retrieve argument array size
	$number_of_arguments = scalar (@_);
	#Print arguments using foreach loop
	print ("\n\nDisplaying arguments using foreach loop.\n");
	foreach $arg (@_)
	{
		print ("\n$arg");
	}
	#Print arguments using any other loop, for that you need argument array size
	#Individual elements of the @_ can be accessed as $_[<index>]
	print ("\n\nDisplaying arguments using while loop.\n\n");
	$count = 0 ;
	#Loop from 0 to 1 less than $number_of_arguments
	while ($count < $number_of_arguments)
	{
		print ("\Argument Number: ", $count + 1, "\tArgument Value: $_[$count]\n");
		#Increment count
		$count ++;
	}
}
#Execution of the script begins here
#Call ShowValue, pass some numbers as arguments
ShowValues(5, -7, 2, 0.784, -3.23, 15);
```

Output:

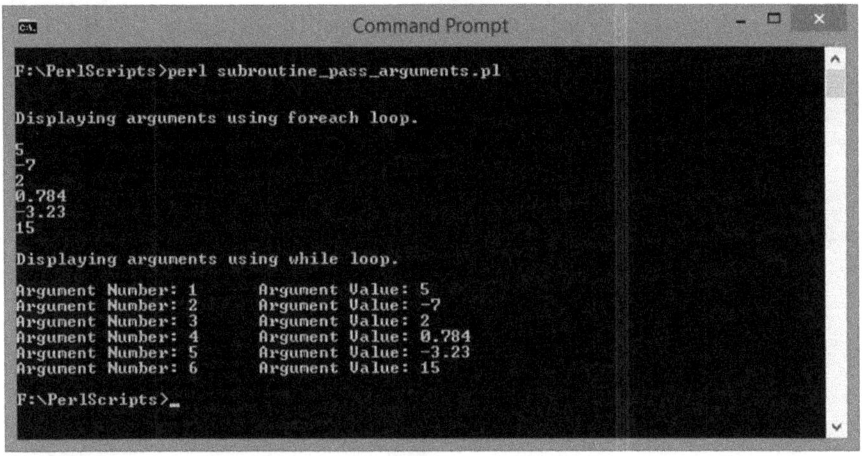

```
Command Prompt

F:\PerlScripts>perl subroutine_pass_arguments.pl

Displaying arguments using foreach loop.

5
-7
2
0.784
-3.23
15

Displaying arguments using while loop.

Argument Number: 1      Argument Value: 5
Argument Number: 2      Argument Value: -7
Argument Number: 3      Argument Value: 2
Argument Number: 4      Argument Value: 0.784
Argument Number: 5      Argument Value: -3.23
Argument Number: 6      Argument Value: 15

F:\PerlScripts>_
```

13.4 Returning a value

A function can return a value back to the calling statement. For example, you can have a function to calculate the average of 5 numbers, pass 5 arguments to it, the function does its job and returns the average to the statement which made the call. Inside the function definition, the ***return*** statement is used to return a value. It is possible to return scalars, arrays and hashes. General syntax:

return <variable>;

Example:

return $average;

At the time of calling this function, there should be a variable to receive the returned value. Without it, the statement will be syntactically correct but the returned value will get lost and you may run into logical issues with the script. General syntax:

<variable> = <function name> (<argument 1>, … <argument n>);

Example:

$avg = findAvg (5, 8, 1, 9, 3);

Here is a Perl script that shows the concept of returning a value:

```
#Subroutine Demo - Passing Arguments and Returning a
value
#We'll have a subroutine that accepts arguments,
calculates sum and returns it
#Subroutine definition
sub FindSum
{
	#Initialize a variable to store sum
	$sum = 0;
	#Iterate through the array of arguments @_
	foreach $arg (@_)
	{
		$sum = $sum + $arg;
	}
	#Return sum
	return $sum;
}
#Execution begins here
#Use a variable to receive returned value
$s = FindSum(3, 1, 88.5, 34, -7, 4.67);
print ("\nThe sum is: $s\n");
```

<u>Output:</u>

Let us now write a script where we will have multiple functions in a single file. We will use a mix of functions that return values, functions that do not return values and also demonstrate one function calling another:

```
#Demo on having multiple functions
#Function to calculate sum of two numbers and return it
sub getSum
{
	#Add first and second argument, return sum
```

```
	$sum = $_[0] + $_[1] ;
	return $sum;
}
#Function to calculate difference and print it
sub showDiff
{
	#Subtract from first argument, the second one,
display difference
	$diff = $_[0] - $_[1] ;
	print ("\nDifference: $diff\n");
}
#Function to calculate product of two numbers and return
it
sub getProd
{
	#This function is slightly different.
	#We know that multiplication is successive
addition.
	#Instead of multiplying and returning the product,
we will call getSum successively
	$prod = 0;
	$neg_flag_1 = 0;
	$neg_flag_2 = 0;
	$arg_1 = $_[0];
	$arg_2 = $_[1];
	if (($arg_1 < 0) ||($arg_2 < 0))
	{
		if ($arg_1 < 0)
		{
			$neg_flag_1 = 1;
			$arg_1 = $arg_1 * -1;
		}
		if ($arg_2 < 0)
		{
			$neg_flag_2 = 1;
			$arg_2 = $arg_2 * -1;
		}
	}
	for ($i = 1 ; $i <= $arg_2 ; $i++)
	{
		$prod = getSum($prod, $arg_1);
	}
	if (($neg_flag_1) || ($neg_flag_2))
	{
		if (($neg_flag_1 == 1) && ($neg_flag_2 ==
1))
		{
```

```
                        $prod = $prod * 1;
                }
                else
                {
                        $prod = $prod * -1;
                }
        }
        return $prod;
}
#Divide two numbers and show quotient
sub divide
{
        $q = $_[0] / $_[1];
        print ("\nQuotient: $q\n");
}
#Execution begins here
#Define arbitrary variables
$a = 20;
$b = 51;
print ("\n\$a = $a \t\$b = $b\n");
#Call functions one by one
$s = getSum($a, $b);
print ("\nSum: $sum\n");
showDiff($a, $b);
$p = getProd($a, $b);
print ("\nProduct: $p\n");
divide($a, $b);
```

Output:

```
Command Prompt

F:\PerlScripts>perl multiplesubroutines.pl
$a = 20         $b = 51
Sum: 71
Difference: -31
Product: 1020
Quotient: 0.392156862745098
F:\PerlScripts>
```

14. Strings

A string is a sequence of characters. We have dealt strings all throughout this book. In this section, we will revise what we have already know and learn more about strings.

14.1 String Basics

A string can be created by enclosing a sequence of characters within single quotes or double quotes but not in a mixed fashion. Meaning, a string cannot start with a single quote and end with double quotes or vice-versa. General Syntax:

> *$<var> = '<sequence of characters>';*
>
> #OR
>
> *$<var> = "<sequence of characters>";*
>
> *Example:*
>
> *$name = "Jason";*
>
> #OR
>
> *$city = 'Glasgow';*

There are several restricted special characters that you cannot directly use such as ***$, @, etc***. If you want to use such characters in your string, you have to make use of the escape character ***backslash (\\)*** and the escape character sequence will become ***\\<restricted character>.*** Example: ***\\$, \\@, etc.***

Note: Escape sequence will only work for strings enclosed within double quotes.

The length of a string can be determined using the ***length()*** function. Syntax:

$<variable> = length (<string>);

Example:

$l = length ($country);

This function counts the number of characters inside a string and returns it. A variable must be used to receive the returned value.

14.2 String Concatenation and Repetition

Two or more strings can be joined together using the concatenation operators given by – ***dot (.)***. General Syntax:

$<var> = $<string 1> . $<string 2>;

Example:

$name = $first_name . " " . $last_name;

A string can be repeated multiple number of times using the repetition operator given by ***x***. General syntax:

$<var> = <string> x <number of times the string should repeat>;

Example:

$str = "Wow" x 3;

Let us write a program to demonstrate these concepts:

```
#String Demo
#Declare a few strings
$str1 = "This is a string declared using double quotes
\" \n";
$str2 = 'This is a string declared using single quotes
\' ';
print ("\n$str1\n$str2\n");
$str3 = "This is just a string.";
$str4 = "This is another string.";
$str5 = "Why do we have so many strings?";
print ("\n$str3\n$str3\n$str4\n");
#Concatenate using + and .
```

```
$str6 = $str3 . " " . $str4 . " " . $str5;
print ("\n$str6\n");
$len = length ($str6);
print ("\nLength of the previous string: $len\n");
$str7 = "Hello World!!! " x 5;
print ("\n$str7\n");
```

Output:

```
Command Prompt
F:\PerlScripts>perl stringdemo1.pl

This is a string declared using double quotes "

This is a string declared using single quotes '

This is just a string.
This is just a string.
This is another string.

This is just a string. This is another string. Why do we have so many strings?

Length of the previous string: 78

Hello World!!! Hello World!!! Hello World!!! Hello World!!! Hello World!!!

F:\PerlScripts>_
```

14.3 Search within a string

A string can be searched within another string using the functions – ***index()*** and ***rindex()***. The ***index()*** function returns the first occurrence of the string while ***rindex()*** function gives the last occurrence of the string. General syntax:

$<var> = index (<source string>, <string to be searched>);

$<var> = rindex (<source string>, <string to be searched>);

Example:

$a = index ("This is just a string", "is");

$b = rindex ($address, "street");

Here is a Perl script that shows string search in action:

```
#String Search Demo
print ("\nEnter a string: ");
#Use prompt to receive the input in the variable $str1
```

```
#Use chomp at the time of taking input.
chomp ($str1 = <STDIN>);
#Ask the user to enter age
print ("\nEnter another string: ");
#Use prompt to receive the input in the variable $str2
#Use chomp at the time of taking input.
chomp ($str2 = (<STDIN>));
#Search for the first occurance of $str2 in $str1 using
index()
$p = index ($str1, $str2);
#Search for the last occurance of $str2 in $str1 using
rindex()
$q = rindex ($str1, $str2);
if (($p == -1) || ($q == -1))
{
      print ("\n$str2 is not found in $str1.\n");
}
else
{
      print  ("\n$str2  has  been  found.  \n\nFirst
occurance: $p, Last occurrence: $q.\n ");
}
```

Output:

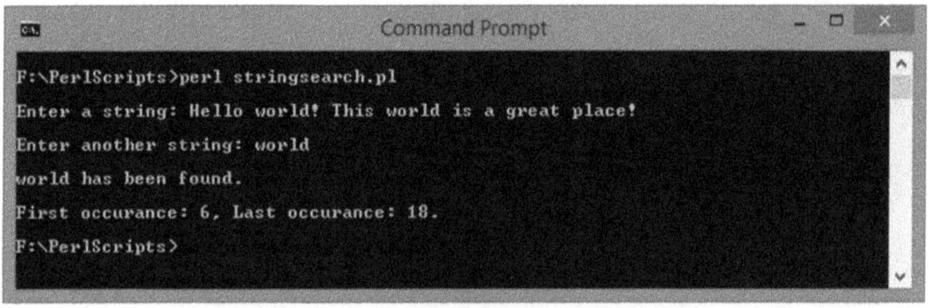

```
F:\PerlScripts>perl stringsearch.pl
Enter a string: Hello world! This world is a great place!
Enter another string: world
world has been found.
First occurance: 6, Last occurance: 18.
F:\PerlScripts>
```

15. File Handling

The concepts we have learned so far involve dealing with hardcoded data or interacting with the user via console. In this section, we will see how to exchange data with local files. File I/O is a huge topic that if covered in full would have occupied 50% of this book. Keeping this mind, I have covered the basics and important concepts. Also, there are a few pointers in this chapter using which you can learn more things about files. We will only deal with plain text files.

VERY IMPORTANT NOTE: When dealing with files, you should have the correct permissions to the directory where your files will be present. It is best to have administrator rights. Without the right permissions, your file operations will fail.

15.1 Basics of File I/O

When dealing with files in Perl, the most important concept is – ***file handle***. A ***file handle*** is like a pointer to a file which can be used to programmatically access the file in question. A scalar variable of any allowed name can be used as a file handle.

15.1.1 Open Files

Opening a file in programmatic terms means that there is some element in the program which is correctly pointing to a file and has internally opened the file. Opening a file does not automatically mean reading it. This is very important. To open a file, we can use the ***open*** function. There are many ways to use this function but we will follow the following syntax for simplicity:

open ([<file handle>], [mode], [file name]);

Example:

open ($file_handle, "<", "my_file.txt");

There are many things that can go wrong while working with files and hence it is recommended that exceptions that can arise during runtime be handled. Exception handling is a vast and advanced topic again and hence it is not covered in this book. For us, all we have to know is – in case something goes wrong while working with a file, what do we do? The answer to that question is – use ***die*** function. We will use the following syntax as a template for opening files throughout this chapter:

open ([<file handle>], [mode], [file name]) or die "<Error Message">;

Example:

open ($file_handle, "<", "my_file.txt") or die "Could not open file";

15.1.2 File Modes

There are different file modes for different purposes such as reading, writing, appending, etc. Here is a list of all the file modes that are available:

Mode	Description
"<"	Opens file for reading only.
">"	Creates a new file for writing. If the file already exists, its contents will be cleared after opening.
">>"	Creates a file for appending. If it does not exist, a new file will be created.
"+<"	Works only with existing files. Can be used for both reading and writing.
"+>"	If the file does not exist, a new one will be created, its contents will be cleared. Can be used for reading and writing.
"+>>"	If the file does not exist, a new one will be created. Can be used for reading and appending.

15.1.3 Close Files

Once a file is opened and operations are performed (like read, write, etc. which will be covered in the sections to follow), it must be closed. The ***close*** function is used in the following way:

close ([file handle]);

Example:

close ($fh);

You can alternatively use this function alongside the ***die*** function as follows:

close ([file handle]) or die "Could not close file";

Example:

close ($fh) or die or die "Could not close file";

15.1.4 Create a simple file

If we open a file with writing mode and close it, an empty file will be created. Here is a script that does this:

```
#File Create Demo
#Note: You will need write permissions to the directory
where the file is to be created.
#Perl supports absolute and relative paths
#If only file name is specified, it will be created in
the CWD

#Set the file name
$file_name = "file_1.txt";
#Open file
open($file_handle, '>', $file_name) or die "Could not
open file '$file_name' $!";
print ("\n$file_name has been created.\n");
#Close file
close($file_handle);
```

Output:

```
Command Prompt
F:\PerlScripts>perl create_file.pl
file_1.txt has been created.
F:\PerlScripts>
```

You can cross-check with the ***dir*** command on Windows and ***ls*** command on Linux/MAC:

```
Command Prompt
F:\PerlScripts>perl create_file.pl
file_1.txt has been created.
F:\PerlScripts>dir file_1*
 Volume in drive F is Data
 Volume Serial Number is

 Directory of F:\PerlScripts

16-03-2020  19:51                 0 file_1.txt
               1 File(s)              0 bytes
               0 Dir(s)  137,125,191,680 bytes free

F:\PerlScripts>
```

As seen, the file is created and its size is 0 bytes. That is because, there is nothing in it.

15.1.5 Writing to a file

Once a file is opened, it can be written to using the ***print*** function. So far, we have used the ***print*** function to print data on the console. What used to happen there is, the ***print*** function by default used to send the output to ***STDOUT***. When writing to a file, we have to specify the file handle that we used at the time of opening the file. With this, the output will now be directed to the file instead of the console. Here is the general syntax:

open ([<file handle>], [mode], [file name]) or die "<Error Message">;

print ([<file handle>] <text/ data>);

Example:

open ($file_handle, ">", "my_file.txt") or die "Could not open file";

print ($file_handle "Hello World!!!");

close ($file_handle);

Here is a Perl script that opens a file, writes some strings to it and closes it:

```
#File Write Demo
#Note: You will need write permissions to the directory
where the file is to be created.
#Perl supports absolute and relative paths
#If only file name is specified, it will be created in
the CWD

#Set the file name
$file_name = "file_2.txt";
#Open file
open($file_handle, '>', $file_name) or die "Could not
open file '$file_name' $!";
print ("\n$file_name has been created.\n");
#Write to the file by directing print function's output
to the $file_handle
print ($file_handle "This is a write test!");
print ($file_handle "\nThis is another line written to
$file_name programmatically.\n");
print ("\nContent has been written to the file. Open in
a text editor.\n");
#Close file
close($file_handle);
```

<u>Output:</u>

```
Command Prompt
F:\PerlScripts>perl write_file.pl
file_2.txt has been created.
Content has been written to the file. Open in a text editor.
F:\PerlScripts>
```

The program tells us that the file has been created and data has been written to. Here is what the file looks like when opened in a text editor:

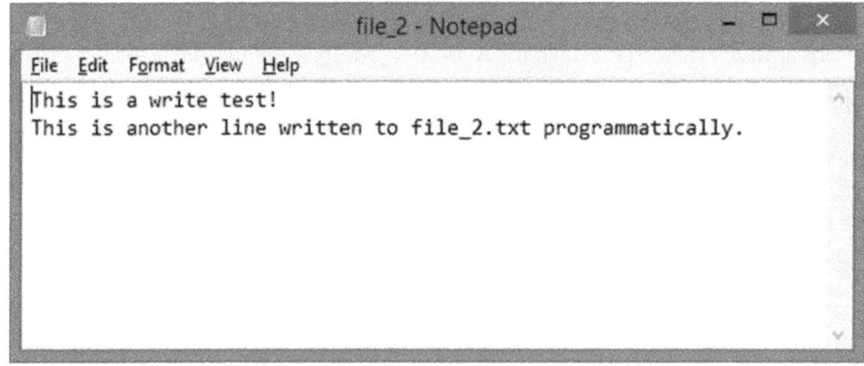
file_2 - Notepad
File Edit Format View Help
This is a write test!
This is another line written to file_2.txt programmatically.

Let us now write a Perl script to take input from the user via prompt and write it to a file:

```
#User input/Write file combined
#Note: You will need write permissions to the directory
where the file is to be created.
#Perl supports absolute and relative paths
#If only file name is specified, it will be created in
the CWD
#Set the file name
$file_name = "user_data.txt";
#Open file
open($file_handle, '>', $file_name) or die "Could not
open file '$file_name' $!";
print ("\n$file_name has been created.\n");
#Loop for 3 times, ask the user to enter name, age and
country of 3 people
for ($i = 1 ; $i <= 3 ; $i++)
{
      #Ask the user to enter name
      print ("\n$i. Enter name: ");
      #Use prompt to receive the input in the variable
$name
      #Use chomp at the time of taking input.
      chomp ($name = <STDIN>);
      #Ask the user to enter age
      print ("\n$i. Enter age: ");
```

```
        #Use prompt to receive the input in the variable
$age
        #Use chomp at the time of taking input.
        chomp ($age = (<STDIN>));
        #Ask the user to enter country
        print ("\n$i. Enter country: ");
        #Use prompt to receive the input in the variable
$country
        #Use chomp at the time of taking input.
        chomp ($country = (<STDIN>));
        #Write to the file by directing print function's
output to the $file_handle
        print ($file_handle "Name: $name");
        print ($file_handle "\nAge: $age");
        print ($file_handle "\nCountry: $country\n\n");
}
#Close file
close($file_handle);
print ("\nThe entered data has been successfully written
to $file_name\n");
```

Output:

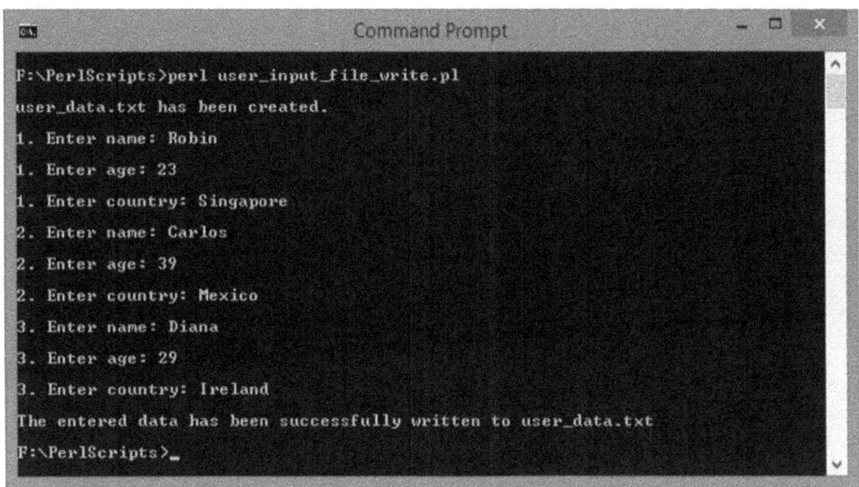

Command Prompt
F:\PerlScripts>perl user_input_file_write.pl
user_data.txt has been created.
1. Enter name: Robin
1. Enter age: 23
1. Enter country: Singapore
2. Enter name: Carlos
2. Enter age: 39
2. Enter country: Mexico
3. Enter name: Diana
3. Enter age: 29
3. Enter country: Ireland
The entered data has been successfully written to user_data.txt
F:\PerlScripts>_

Here is what ***user_data.txt*** file looks like:

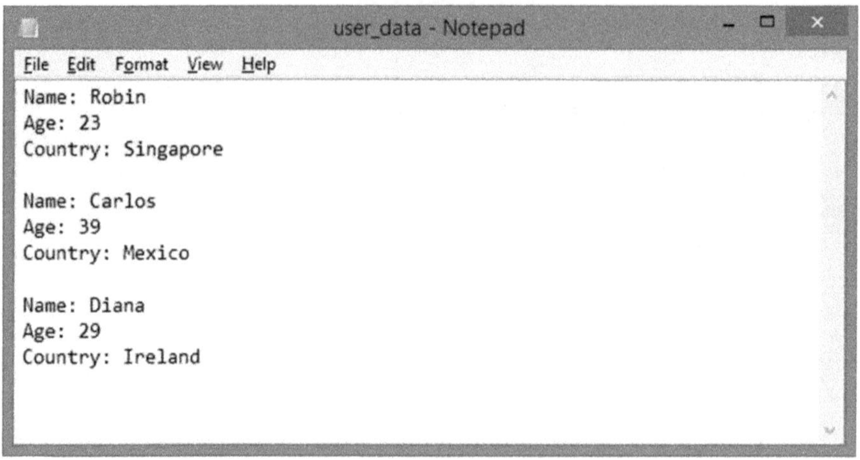

15.1.6 Reading from a file

In order to read text from a file, we need to use the ***diamond operator (<>)*** over the file handle once the file is opened. The empty diamond operator reads input from the STDIN, which is keyboard while the diamond operator used over the file handle will read from the file. If you try to print ***<[file handle]>*** using the ***print*** function, all the contents of the file will be printed. Here is a script that reads from ***user_data.txt*** created by a program in the previous section:

```
#Read file demo
#Note: You will need read permissions to the directory
from where the file is to be read.
#Perl supports absolute and relative paths
#If only file name is specified, it will be created in
the CWD
#Set the file name
$file_name = "user_data.txt";
#Open file
open($file_handle, '<', $file_name) or die "Could not
open file '$file_name' $!";
print ("\n$file_name has been opened for reading.\n");
print ("\nFile content:\n\n");
print (<$file_handle>);
#Close file
close($file_handle);
```

Output:

```
F:\PerlScripts>perl read_file.pl
user_data.txt has been opened for reading.
File content:
Name: Robin
Age: 23
Country: Singapore

Name: Carlos
Age: 39
Country: Mexico

Name: Diana
Age: 29
Country: Ireland

F:\PerlScripts>_
```

If you want to read the file line by line, you can use a loop to iterate over the file handle using the diamond operator. For example:

while (<$file_handle>)

{

#Do something…

}

During each iteration, the loop will fetch the next line. The current line will be given by the special variable ***$_***. Here is a script that reads ***user_data.txt*** line by line:

```
#Read file demo
#Note: You will need read permissions to the directory
from where the file is to be read.
#Perl supports absolute and relative paths
#If only file name is specified, it will be created in
the CWD
#Set the file name
$file_name = "user_data.txt";
#Open file
open($file_handle, '<', $file_name) or die "Could not
open file '$file_name' $!";
print ("\n$file_name has been opened for reading.\n");
print ("\nFile content line by line:\n\n");
#Loop until <$file_handle> has data
```

```
$line_number = 1;
while (<$file_handle>)
{
      print ($line_number, ". ", $_);
      $line_number++;
}
#Close file
close($file_handle);
```

Output:

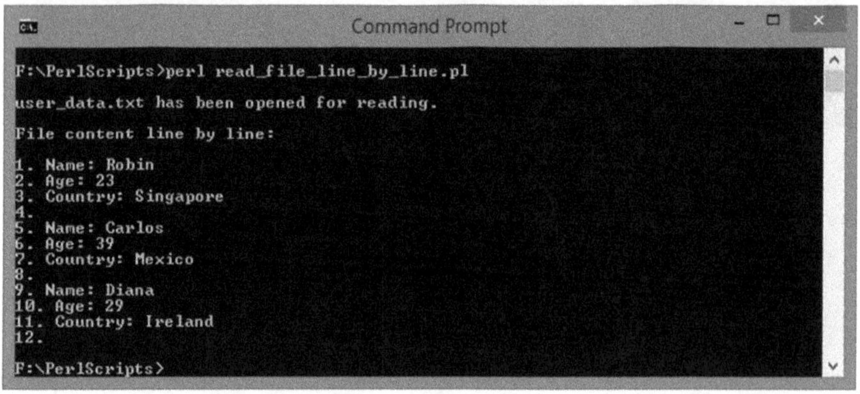

```
Command Prompt
F:\PerlScripts>perl read_file_line_by_line.pl
user_data.txt has been opened for reading.
File content line by line:
1. Name: Robin
2. Age: 23
3. Country: Singapore
4.
5. Name: Carlos
6. Age: 39
7. Country: Mexico
8.
9. Name: Diana
10. Age: 29
11. Country: Ireland
12.
F:\PerlScripts>
```

15.1.7 Search text inside a file

Let us write a Perl script to search text inside a file. To accomplish this, we will open a file, ask the user to enter a string to be searched inside the file. We will then read this file line by line and check if the entered substring is present in any of the lines. We will again use ***user_data.txt*** file as our source file.

```
#Read file, search for text
#Note: You will need read permissions to the directory
from where the file is to be read.
#Perl supports absolute and relative paths
#If only file name is specified, it will be created in
the CWD
#Set the file name
$file_name = "user_data.txt";
#Open file
open($file_handle, '<', $file_name) or die "Could not
open file '$file_name' $!";
```

```
print ("\n$file_name has been opened for reading.\n");
#Ask the user to enter string to be searched
print ("\nEnter a string: ");
#Use prompt to receive the input in the variable $str
#Use chomp at the time of taking input.
chomp ($str = <STDIN>);
#Loop until <$file_handle> has data
$line_number = 1;
$found = -1;
while (<$file_handle>)
{
	#Search for the first occurance of $str in $_ using
index()
	$p = index ($_, $str);
	#Search for the last occurance of $str in $_ using
rindex()
	$q = rindex ($_, $str);
	if (($p == -1) || ($q == -1))
	{
		#Do nothing here
	}
	else
	{
		print ("\nLine: $line_number, $str has been
found. \n\nFirst occurance: $p, Last occurance: $q.\n
");
		$found = 1;
	}
	$line_number++;
}
if ($found == -1)
{
	print ("\nThe entered string was not found.\n");
}
#Close file
close($file_handle);
```

Output:

Command Prompt
F:\PerlScripts>perl search_in_a_file.pl
user_data.txt has been opened for reading.
Enter a string: Ireland
Line: 11, Ireland has been found.
First occurance: 9, Last occurance: 9.
F:\PerlScripts>perl search_in_a_file.pl
user_data.txt has been opened for reading.
Enter a string: Thailand
The entered string was not found.
F:\PerlScripts>_

16. Programming Examples

Let us put the concepts we have learned so far to the test and write some Perl scripts.

16.1 Prime or Composite

```
#Check if a number is prime or composite
print ("\nEnter a number: ");
#Use prompt to receive the input in the variable $num
#Use chomp at the time of taking input.
chomp ($num = (<>));
$prime_flag = 0;
for ($i = 2; $i < $num ; $i++ )
{
        if ($num%$i == 0)
        {
                $prime_flag = 1;
                last;
        }
}
if (!($prime_flag))
{
        print ("\n$num is prime.\n");
}
else
{
        print ("\n$num is composite.\n");
}
```

Output:

```
Command Prompt
F:\PerlScripts>perl primeorcomposite.pl
Enter a number: 5
5 is prime.
F:\PerlScripts>perl primeorcomposite.pl
Enter a number: 17
17 is prime.
F:\PerlScripts>perl primeorcomposite.pl
Enter a number: 49
49 is composite.
F:\PerlScripts>_
```

16.2 Fibonacci Series

Let us write a Perl script to generate ***Fibonacci Series*** where in the next term is given by current term plus previous term. It starts with the first two terms 0 and 1. The next terms are 1, 2, 3, 5, 8 and so on. Here is the script:

```
#Fibonacci series
print ("\nEnter the number of terms to be generated: ");
#Use prompt to receive the input in the variable $num
#Use chomp at the time of taking input.
chomp ($num = (<>));
$prev = 0;
$current = 1;
print ("\nFibonacci Series: \n\n");
#Generate Fibo series
print ($prev, " ", $current, " ");
for ($i = 0 ; $i < $num - 1 ; $i++)
{
	$next = $prev + $current ;
	print ($next, " ");
	$prev = $current;
	$current = $next;
}
print ("\n");
```

Output:

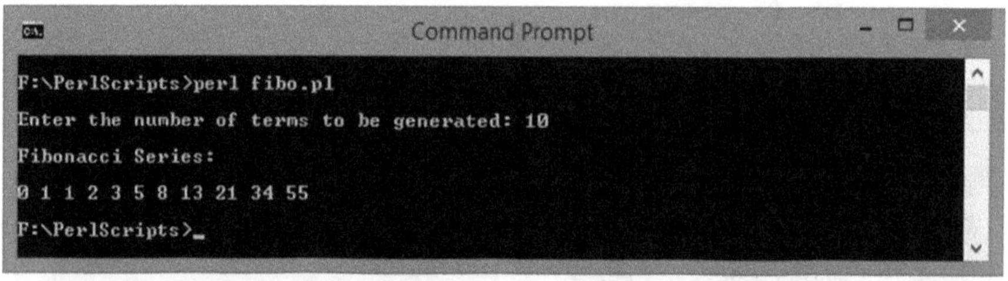

```
F:\PerlScripts>perl fibo.pl
Enter the number of terms to be generated: 10
Fibonacci Series:
0 1 1 2 3 5 8 13 21 34 55
F:\PerlScripts>_
```

16.3 Sum of digits of a number

Let us write a Perl script to accept a number as an input from the user and calculate the sum of all the digits of the number. To do so, we will have to retrieve the digit at one's place and discard it progressively by dividing the number by 10 and taking only the integer part using the *int* function.

```
#Sum of all the digits of a number
print ("\nEnter a number: ");
#Use prompt to receive the input in the variable $number
#Use chomp at the time of taking input.
chomp ($number = (<>));
$sum = 0;
while ( $number > 0 )
{
		#Add one's place digit to $sum
		$sum = $sum + ( $number % 10 ) ;
		#Discard one's place digit. int function
will return only the integer part
		$number = int ($number / 10) ;
}
print ("\nSum of digits: $sum\n");
```

Output:

```
Command Prompt
F:\PerlScripts>perl sumofdigits.pl
Enter a number: 1234
Sum of digits: 10
F:\PerlScripts>_
```

16.4 Reverse a number

Here is a Perl script that accepts a number from the user and reverses it:

```
#Sum of all the digits of a number
print ("\nEnter a number: ");
#Use prompt to receive the input in the variable $number
#Use chomp at the time of taking input.
chomp ($number = (<>));
$rev = 0;
while ( $number > 0 )
{
		#Multiply 10 to $rev to take the reverse to
the next place
		#Add one's digit to rev
```

```
            $rev = ($rev * 10 ) + ( $number % 10 ) ;
            #Discard one's digit. Use int function
            $number = int ($number / 10) ;
}
print ("\nReverse: $rev\n");
```

Output:

```
F:\PerlScripts>perl reversenum.pl
Enter a number: 12345
Reverse: 54321
F:\PerlScripts>_
```

16.5 Menu driven program

Let us write a menu driven Perl script to add, subtract, multiply and divide two numbers. We will write functions for each of these operations.

```
#Menu driven program
#Function to find sum
sub getSum
{
        $sum = $_[0] + $_[1];
        return $sum;
}
#Function to find difference
sub getDiff
{
        $diff = $_[0] - $_[1];
        return $diff;
}
#Function to find product
sub getProd
{
        $prod = $_[0] * $_[1];
        return $prod;
}
#Function to find quotient
sub getQuotient
{
        $q = ($_[0]/$_[1]);
```

```
        return $q;
}
#Execution begins here
while (1)
{
        print   ("\n1.   Addition\n2.   Subtraction\n3.
Multiplication\n4. Division\n5. Quit");
        print ("\n\nEnter your choice: ");
        #Use prompt to receive the input in the variable
$choice
        #Use chomp at the time of taking input.
        chomp ($choice = (<>));
        if ($choice == 5)
        {
                last;
        }
        print ("\nEnter x: ");
        #Use prompt to receive the input in the variable
$x
        #Use chomp at the time of taking input.
        chomp ($x = (<>));
        print ("\nEnter y: ");
        #Use prompt to receive the input in the variable
$y
        #Use chomp at the time of taking input.
        chomp ($y = (<>));
        if ($choice == 1)
        {
                $s = getSum ($x, $y);
                print ("\nSum = $s\n");
        }
        elsif ($choice == 2)
        {
                $d = getDiff ($x, $y);
                print ("\nDiff = $d\n");
        }
        elsif ($choice == 3)
        {
                $p = getProd ($x, $y);
                print ("\nProd = $p\n");
        }
        elsif ($choice == 4)
        {
                $q = getQuotient ($x, $y);
                print ("\nQuotient = $q\n");
        }
}
```

Output:

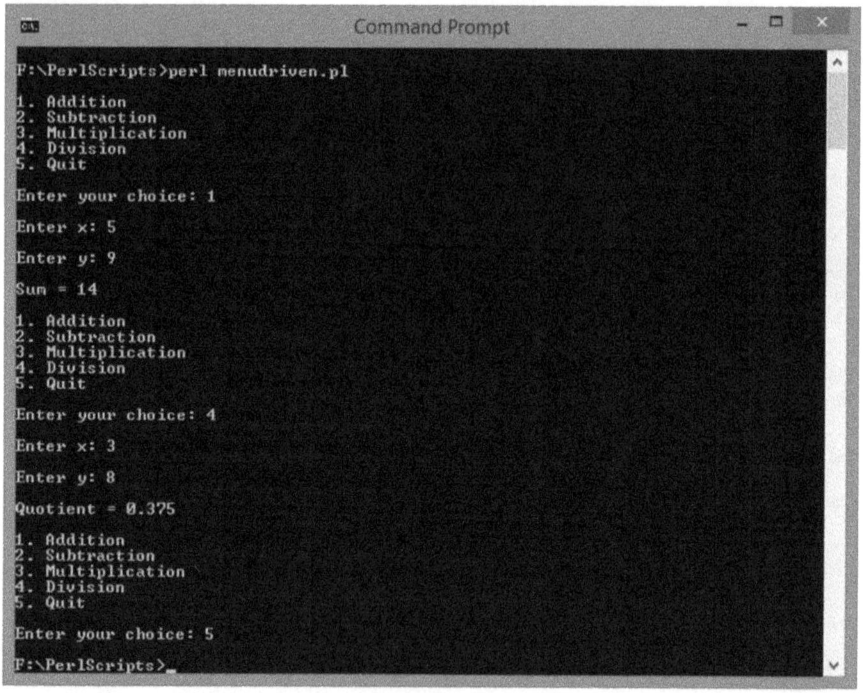

```
F:\PerlScripts>perl menudriven.pl

1. Addition
2. Subtraction
3. Multiplication
4. Division
5. Quit

Enter your choice: 1

Enter x: 5

Enter y: 9

Sum = 14

1. Addition
2. Subtraction
3. Multiplication
4. Division
5. Quit

Enter your choice: 4

Enter x: 3

Enter y: 8

Quotient = 0.375

1. Addition
2. Subtraction
3. Multiplication
4. Division
5. Quit

Enter your choice: 5

F:\PerlScripts>_
```

16.6 Lowest Common Multiple

Let us write a program to determine the LCM of two numbers:

```
#LCM
print ("\nEnter a number: ");
#Use prompt to receive the input in the variable $x
#Use chomp at the time of taking input.
chomp ($x = (<>));
print ("\nEnter another number: ");
#Use prompt to receive the input in the variable $y
#Use chomp at the time of taking input.
chomp ($y = (<>));
if ($x > $y)
{
        $lcm = $x;
}
else
{
        $lcm = $y;
```

```
}
#Run while loop infinitely, break when LCM if found
while(1)
{
	if( ($lcm % $x == 0) && ($lcm % $y == 0) )
	{
	 print ("\nLCM: $lcm\n");
	 last;
	}
	$lcm = $lcm + 1;
}
```

Output:

```
Command Prompt
F:\PerlScripts>perl lcm.pl
Enter a number: 12
Enter another number: 8
LCM: 24
F:\PerlScripts>_
```

16.7 Search for an element in an array

There are various algorithms to search for elements in an array. We will implement the simplest one called as linear search. In this algorithm, the search begins at index 0 and goes up to (size – 1). If the element is found, we come out of the loop. Only the first occurrence of the element will be reported.

```
#Implement linear search
#Create a blank array
@arr = ();
#Create a flag
$flag_found = 0;
$i = 0;
#Run for loop 5 times
for ($i = 0 ; $i < 5 ; $i++)
{
	print ("\nEnter element at index $i: ");
	#Read input, chomp it
	chomp ($num = (<>));
```

```
        #Store it in the array
        $arr[$i] = $num;
}
#Display the array
for ($i = 0 ; $i < 5 ; $i++)
{
        print ("\nIndex: $i\t\@arr[$i] = $arr[$i]");
}
print ("\n\nEnter the element to be searched: ");
chomp ($x = (<>));
#Begin search
for ($i = 0 ; $i < 5 ; $i++)
{
        if (($x == $arr[$i]))
        {
                $flag_found = 1;
                last;
        }
}
if ($flag_found)
{
        print ("\nThe element $x has been found at $i.\n");
}
else
{
        print ("\nThe element $x is not present in the
array.\n");
}
```

Output:

```
Command Prompt

F:\PerlScripts>perl linearsearch.pl
Enter element at index 0: 12
Enter element at index 1: -5
Enter element at index 2: 3
Enter element at index 3: -9
Enter element at index 4: 15
Index: 0        @arr[0] = 12
Index: 1        @arr[1] = -5
Index: 2        @arr[2] = 3
Index: 3        @arr[3] = -9
Index: 4        @arr[4] = 15
Enter the element to be searched: 3
The element 3 has been found at 2.
F:\PerlScripts>
```

16.8 Greatest element in an array

In order to find the greatest element in an array, we start at index 0, assume that the first element is the greatest. If we find a greater element than our greatest, we make that element greatest during the course of loop iterations.

```
#Greatest in an array
#Create a blank array
@arr = ();
#Run for loop 5 times
for ($i = 0 ; $i < 5 ; $i++)
{
	print ("\nEnter element at index $i: ");
	#Read input, chomp it
	chomp ($num = (<>));
	#Store it in the array
	$arr[$i] = $num;
}
#Display the array
for ($i = 0 ; $i < 5 ; $i++)
{
	print ("\nIndex: $i\t\@arr[$i] = $arr[$i]");
}
#Assume first number is the greatest
$greatest = $arr[0];
#Find greatest
for ($i = 0 ; $i < 5 ; $i++)
{
	#If current element is greater than greatest, make
it greatest
	if ($arr[$i] > $greatest)
	{
		$greatest = $arr[$i];
	}
}
print ("\n\nGreatest element: $greatest\n");
```

Output:

```
F:\PerlScripts>perl array_greatest.pl

Enter element at index 0: 99

Enter element at index 1: -45

Enter element at index 2: 193

Enter element at index 3: -56

Enter element at index 4: 23

Index: 0        @arr[0] = 99
Index: 1        @arr[1] = -45
Index: 2        @arr[2] = 193
Index: 3        @arr[3] = -56
Index: 4        @arr[4] = 23

Greatest element: 193

F:\PerlScripts>_
```

16.9 Bubble Sort

Bubble sort is an array sorting algorithm where an element is compared to the next one. If the current element is greater than the next one, the elements are swapped. During each iteration, the greatest element reaches the end of the array.

```
#Bubble Sort
#Create a blank array
@arr = ();
$size = 5;
#Run for loop 5 times
for ($i = 0 ; $i < $size ; $i++)
{
	print ("\nEnter element at index $i: ");
	#Read input, chomp it
	chomp ($num = (<>));
	#Store it in the array
	$arr[$i] = $num;
}
#Display the array
print ("\n\nUnsorted array:\n");
for ($i = 0 ; $i < $size ; $i++)
{
	print ("\nIndex: $i\t\@arr[$i] = $arr[$i]");
}
#Core of bubble sort algorith
```

```
for ($i = 0 ; $i < $size ; $i++)
{
	for ($j = 0 ; $j < ($size - $i - 1) ; $j++)
	{
		if ($arr[$j] > $arr[$j+1])
		{
			$temp = $arr[$j];
			$arr[$j] = $arr[$j+1];
			$arr[$j+1] = $temp;
		}
	}
}
print ("\n\nSorted array:\n");
for ($i = 0 ; $i < $size ; $i++)
{
	print ("\nIndex: $i\t\@arr[$i] = $arr[$i]");
}
```

Output:

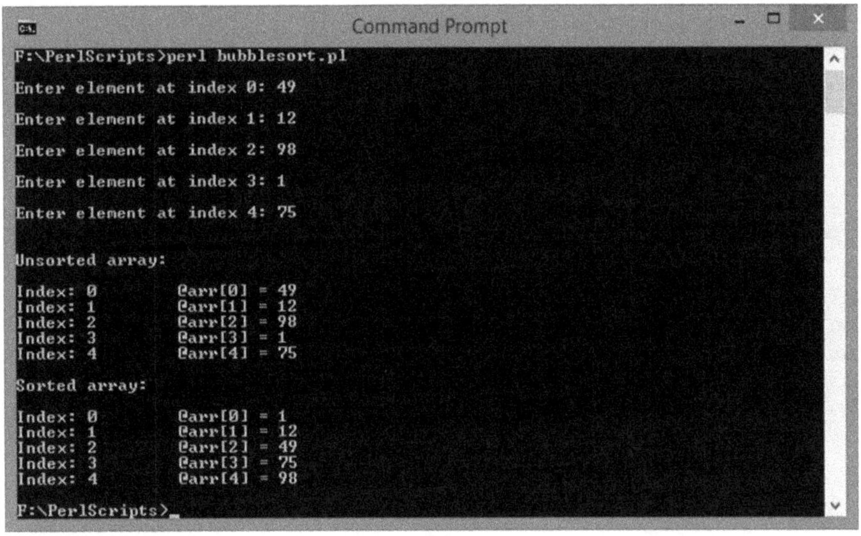

```
Command Prompt
F:\PerlScripts>perl bubblesort.pl

Enter element at index 0: 49

Enter element at index 1: 12

Enter element at index 2: 98

Enter element at index 3: 1

Enter element at index 4: 75


Unsorted array:

Index: 0        @arr[0] = 49
Index: 1        @arr[1] = 12
Index: 2        @arr[2] = 98
Index: 3        @arr[3] = 1
Index: 4        @arr[4] = 75

Sorted array:

Index: 0        @arr[0] = 1
Index: 1        @arr[1] = 12
Index: 2        @arr[2] = 49
Index: 3        @arr[3] = 75
Index: 4        @arr[4] = 98

F:\PerlScripts>_
```

16.10 File Copy

Let us write a Perl script to copy a file. This is not as difficult as it sounds. All we have to do is, open a file. Read it line by line. As we are reading the lines, write those lines to another file. Let us create a source file with arbitrary data. This is what my source file looks like:

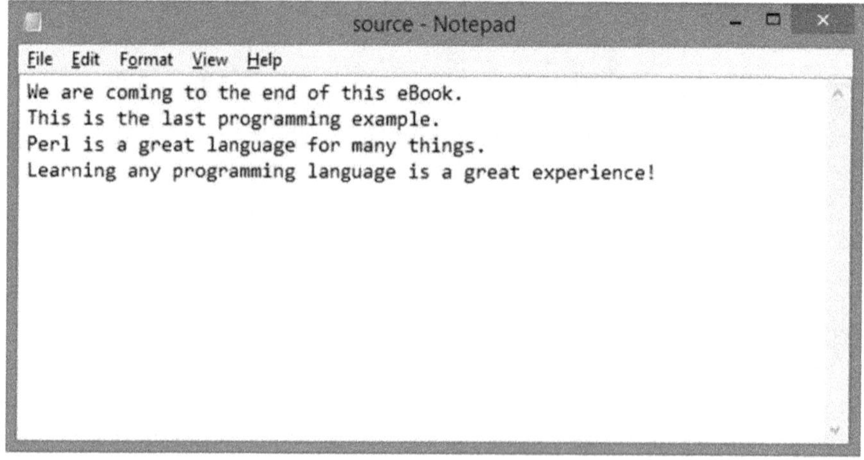

Here is the script:

```
#Copy file demo
#Note: You will need read/write permissions
#Perl supports absolute and relative paths
#If only file name is specified, it will be created in
the CWD
#Set the file names
$file_name_src = "source.txt";
$file_name_dest = "destination.txt";
#Open files
open($file_handle_src, '<', $file_name_src) or die
"Could not open file '$file_name_src' $!";
print ("\n$file_name_src has been opened for
reading.\n");
open($file_handle_dest, '>', $file_name_dest) or die
"Could not open file '$file_name_dest' $!";
print ("\n$file_name_dest has been opened for
writing.\n");
print ("\nFile content line by line:\n\n");
#Loop until <$file_handle> has data
$line_number = 1;
while (<$file_handle_src>)
{
	#Print content to the console
	print ($line_number, ". ", $_);
	#Print line to the file
	print ($file_handle_dest $_);
	$line_number++;
}
```

```
print ("\n\nContent from $file_name_src has been copied
to $file_name_dest\n");
#Close files
close($file_handle_src);
close($file_handle_dest);
```

Output:

```
Command Prompt
F:\PerlScripts>perl copyfile.pl
source.txt has been opened for reading.
destination.txt has been opened for writing.
File content line by line:
1. We are coming to the end of this eBook.
2. This is the last programming example.
3. Perl is a great language for many things.
4. Learning any programming language is a great experience!
Content from source.txt has been copied to destination.txt
F:\PerlScripts>_
```

Here is what the destination file looks like:

```
destination - Notepad
File Edit Format View Help
We are coming to the end of this eBook.
This is the last programming example.
Perl is a great language for many things.
Learning any programming language is a great experience!
```

17. Final Thoughts

This book was meant for beginners and hence I have covered the basics of each chapter and tried to break down concepts as much as possible. Perl is still very useful for a wide variety of things ranging from system administration to web development. In my opinion, Perl is one of the easier scripting languages out there. As a beginner you should get as much hands-on experience as possible. I suggest you try out different programming examples on your own. Change the conditions, challenge yourself and see yourself getting better at programming!

If you have enjoyed this book and want to learn more, there are plenty of resources on the internet. You should dig deeper into more advanced concepts such as exception handling, object oriented programming, web development, etc.

I hope you have learned something of value from this book.

Good Luck!

If you enjoyed this book as much as I've enjoyed writing it, you can subscribe* to my email list for exclusive content and sneak peaks of my future books.

Visit the link below:

http://eepurl.com/du_L4n

OR

Use the QR Code:

(*Must be 13 years or older to subscribe)